NATIONAL GEOGRAPHIC DIRECTIONS

THE EDGE *of* MAINE

THE EDGE *of* MAINE

GEOFFREY WOLFF

NATIONAL GEOGRAPHIC DIRECTIONS

NATIONAL GEOGRAPHIC
Washington, D.C.

Published by the National Geographic Society
1145 17th Street, N.W., Washington, D.C. 20036-4688

Text copyright © 2005 Geoffrey Wolff
Map copyright © 2005 National Geographic Society

Library of Congress Cataloging-in-Publication Data
Wolff, Geoffrey, 1937-
  The edge of Maine / Geoffrey Wolff.
     p. cm. -- (National Geographic directions)
  ISBN 0-7922-3871-0
  1. Atlantic Coast (Me.)--Description and travel. 2. Atlantic Coast (Me.)--History, Local.
3. Maine--Description and travel. 4. Maine--History, Local. 5. Wolff, Geoffrey,
1937---Travel--Maine--Atlantic Coast. I. Title. II. Series.
  F27.A75W65 2005
  917.4--dc22

                                                              2005047905

Interior design by Melissa Farris

Printed in the U.S.A.

For Ivan and Ruby

CONTENTS

THE EDGE *of* MAINE

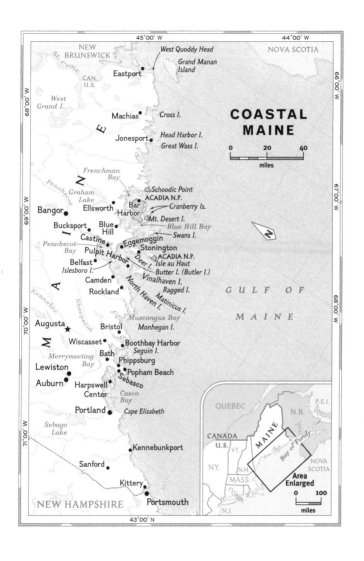

COASTAL MAINE

NEW BRUNSWICK

NOVA SCOTIA

St. Croix

CAN.
U.S.

West
Grand L.

West Quoddy Head

Grand Manan
Island

Eastport

Machias

Cross I.

Jonesport

Head Harbor I.
Great Wass I.

Frenchman
Bay

Penobscot

Graham
Lake

Schoodic Point
ACADIA N.P.

Bar
Harbor

Cranberry Is.

Bangor

Ellsworth

Mt. Desert I.

Bucksport

Blue
Hill

Blue Hill Bay

Castine

Eggemoggin

Swans I.

Penobscot
Bay

Pulpit Harbor

Stonington

ACADIA N.P.

Belfast

Deer I.

Isle au Haut

Islesboro I.

Butter I. (Butler I.)

Vinalhaven I.

Camden

Ragged I.

Rockland

North Haven I.

Matinicus I.

Kennebec

Sheepscot

Muscongus Bay

Monhegan I.

Augusta

Bristol

Wiscasset

Boothbay Harbor

Bath

Seguin I.

Merrymeeting
Bay

Phippsburg

Lewiston

Popham Beach

Auburn

Harpswell
Center

Sebasco

Casco
Bay

Portland

Cape Elizabeth

Sebago
Lake

Kennebunkport

Sanford

Kittery

NEW HAMPSHIRE

Portsmouth

GULF OF

MAINE

0   20   40
miles

N

45°00' W   44°00' W

68°00' W

69°00' W

70°00' W

71°00' W

43°00' N

66°00' W

67°00' W

68°00' W

QUEBEC

P.E.I.

N.B.

CANADA
U.S.

MAINE

Bay of Fundy

VT.

NOVA
SCOTIA

N.Y.

N.H.

MASS.

CONN.

R.I.

Area
Enlarged

0   100
miles

N.J.

NORUMBEGA

John Milton, in Book Ten of *Paradise Lost,* specifies the climatic consequences of man's disobedience to God. Global warming was bad enough, but more theatrical were those cosmic wintry blasts that felled trees and enraged the sea. Freezing winds blew from as far away as frostbit Siberia's northeast coast and marvelous Norumbega:

> *These changes in the heavens, though slow, produced*
> *Like change on sea and land—sidereal blast,*
> *Vapour, and mist, and exhalation hot,*
> *Corrupt and pestilent. Now from the north*
> *Of Norumbega, and the Samoed shore,*
> *Bursting their brazen dungeon, armed with ice,*
> *And snow, and hail, and stormy gust and flaw ...*
> *{Winds loudly} rend the woods, and seas upturn;*

City and kingdom, Norumbega—set at the tidehead of Maine's Penobscot River—rivaled the gold-encrusted capitals of the Inca and Aztec Empires for the fabulous wealth and ingenuity of its people. Samuel Eliot Morison writes that the place-name is Algonquin for "quiet place between two rapids," but "quiet" is an inapt modifier to describe the astonishing settlement's nature and achievement. It was discovered during the sixteenth century by a series of European explorers ranging Maine's coast and rivers; they competed with one another for the extravagance of their reports. Pierre Crignon, writing in 1545, extolled Norumbega's "docile" inhabitants, "friendly and peaceful. The land overflows with every kind of fruit; there grows there the wholesome orange and the almond, and many sorts of sweet-smelling trees." Fourteen years later Jean Alfonce's account of his visit, *La Cosmographie,* offered a more vivid picture of "Norombegue": Here were "clever inhabitants and a mass of peltries of all kinds of beasts. The citizens dress in furs, wearing sable cloaks." Conveniently they spoke a language "which sounds like Latin." Moreover, unlike your commonplace dusky savages, "they are fair people and tall."* But wait: There's more! Morison tells of David Ingram, an English sailor stranded in the Gulf of Mexico in 1567 by the explorer

* Samuel Eliot Morison's *European Discovery of America: the Northern Voyages* has a learned and charming account of Norumbega.

and slave trader Sir Jack Hawkins; Ingram tramped from Yucatan to Down East. In 1569 he was rescued in Newfoundland and returned home to enjoy free drinks telling in many a tavern of his discoveries. This Sinbad's description of Norumbega made so deep an impression on his audience that Richard Hakluyt published Ingram's account in the 1589 edition of his *Principal Navigations*. An impressionable reader—Sir Humfry Gilbert—interviewed Ingram and as a result raised money for an expedition to visit the northwoods Shangri-la. It should have been easy to find, a village half a mile long with streets broader than London's broadest. Norumbega's citizens wore gold and silver hoops on their arms, and these were "garnished with pearls, diverse of them as big as one's thumb"; the natives used these pearls as small change. The women wore plates of gold as armor and counted their gemstones by the bushel. The Norumbegans' round (but somehow turreted) dwellings were supported by "pillars of gold, sylver and crystal" and wallpapered with fur. Elephants lived among penguins and flamingoes, and the happy inhabitants displayed rubies four inches in circumference. Gilbert assured his investors that the pub-crawling Ingram had attested to finding gold nuggets as big as his fist, scattered for the taking (Ingram evidently had forgotten to take any) in small brooks nearby.

Gilbert crossed from England but never found the Penobscot River, let alone Norumbega. In 1604 Samuel de Champlain sailed up that river to the head of navigation. He decided that Ingram was a bullshit artist. He found himself not in what Morison titles the "New Jerusalem" of fevered legend but among a dreary hodgepodge of aboriginal huts in the neighborhood we call Bangor.

Ah, Bangor! Storied hometown of lumberjacks, fur traders, sailors, muggers, tavern keepers, confidence men, and whores: In this very place chewing gum was invented in 1842. Myth has a stranglehold on the little city: Hank and Jan Taft's *A Cruising Guide to the Maine Coast* attests that there's a "birth certificate on file at the Chamber of Commerce" to assure the gullible that Paul Bunyan was born in Bangor on February 12, 1834; the city erected a statue of Bunyan thirty-one feet tall, his exact height in real life, on lower Main Street. Thousands of sailing ships delivered freight to Bangor every year during the boom of the 1860s, and millions of board feet of white pines felled nearby drifted down the Penobscot during river-jamming spring drives.

The marvels of Bangor have exerted a powerful pull. In 1977, a Bavarian brewery worker, en route by charter flight from Hamburg to San Francisco, disembarked at Bangor during a refueling stop. Erwin Kreuz had been aloft all night, and had consumed much of the fruit of his labors; he later confided that he was a seventeen-beer-a-day man. He spoke no English but for three days he toured Bangor in search of the Golden Gate Bridge. The bridge that he found, fording the Penobscot River, made a poor impression on him, but otherwise he liked the town just fine. Like San Francisco, it had water nearby, and hills, and a hotel—Bangor House—where he slept. His navigational error was discovered after a taxicab driver demurred angrily at Kreuz's command that he be driven to "downtown San Francisco," and a tavern waitress who had served the bewildered tourist put him together with a German-speaking Czechoslovakian immigrant. The situation was publicized, and the *San Francisco Examiner* treated the German to a visit to the genuine City by the Bay. Despite attending a rodeo at the Cow Palace and being given an honorary Chinese name by residents of Chinatown, Kreuz revealed to San Francisco's mayor George Moscone that he preferred Maine's version of a port city.

The adventurer received marriage proposals from grateful Down Easters and was made an honorary member of the Penobscot Indian tribe. Now he's welcome to visit the "quiet place between two rapids" whenever he pleases. Upon arriving home at the Frankfurt airport, the returning explorer boasted to an international press contingent: "If Kennedy can claim, 'I am a Berliner,' then I am a Bangor."

EDGING UP ON IT

"We may reason to our heart's content, the fog won't lift."
—SAMUEL BECKETT

I'd first come to the edge of Maine at fourteen from the sky, riding a DC-3 into Bangor a few minutes after a midsummer sunset and then by Pontiac station wagon to Castine. I was visiting a girl I scarcely knew; we'd met during a glee club concert at my school. She was fifteen, an only child, and her dad, driving along the Penobscot River, was asking questions—where did I expect to go to college and did I sail?—and his wife was trying to draw my attention to points of historical and topographical interest out there in the night. In the back seat the girl and I were already holding hands and I wasn't looking out any car windows. After Bucksport the parents clammed up the final half hour as their headlights bounced off streaks of fog swirling at the shoulders of country roads. The station wagon poked hesitantly down a finger of land bounded by the Penobscot and Bagaduce Rivers, to its tip on Perkins Point. The drive must have tired them, because after feeding us hot chocolate in their big country kitchen, they sent us off to bed. My room was upstairs at one end of a long hall with creaky pine floors; their daughter's was at the other end; mommy and daddy slept between, with their door open. The next morning, anxious that I might be called on to show what I'd meant when I'd answered that I "liked" to sail—without mentioning that I had been in a sailboat once in my life, and hadn't been happy to be there—I woke soon after dawn, and before me I saw for the first time one of coastal Maine's representative prospects. The house was set on a bluff above Wadsworth Cove and my bedroom windows were aimed to look across a few miles of Penobscot Bay to Islesboro. The curtains hung still and heavy at my open windows, and for a moment I believed it was drizzling rain from my ceiling. Outside was milky, thick. Whatever sailors did, I reckoned, was not going to be done this morning. I gathered my damp sheets around my damp flannel pajamas and fell back asleep. The fog was as lazy as I; it stayed put the whole week. I had much opportunity to study this fog. Its physical properties—droplets responding sluggishly to gravity and stirred gently by an occasional breeze—were dynamic, but the affective atmosphere of the matter—

gloom, dampness, a shutoff of the world—was static and unrelenting. A couple of days before I was scheduled to leave, my hosts didn't even try to disguise their anxiety: DC-3s weren't flying into or taking off from Bangor. I manfully volunteered to hang around till the murk burned off, but these considerate folks wouldn't hear of monopolizing more of my summer and sent me home by bus. My soi-disant girlfriend seemed stoic about my leave-taking. Rumbling along Route 1 during that long, long journey to New York—past many a roadside enterprise selling garden gnomes or lobster traps, and crossing the occasional bridge with the rumor of water below—I realized that I'd have to wait to "see" that part of Down East beyond the low tide line. Maine was in no hurry to show its stuff to me. Meantime I began Dickens's *Bleak House,* which my hosts had given me as a souvenir:

> *Fog everywhere. Fog up the river, where it flows among green aits and meadows; fog down the river, where it rolls defiled among the tiers of shipping … fog in the stem and bowl of the afternoon pipe of the wrathful skipper, down in his close cabin; fog cruelly pinching toes and fingers of his shivering little 'prentice boy on deck.*

Thirty years later, asked "Do you sail?," I'd respond with a straight face: "Do I sail? Are you kidding?" In 1982, aboard our thirty-foot cutter *Blackwing,* clearing Race Point northwest of Cape Cod's tip at Provincetown, on an offshore course bearing northeast 112 nautical miles for Monhegan Island, my wife asked, "Are you sure you can do this?" I gave the only possible answer.

Priscilla and I had sailed a good deal by then, in the Caribbean and Europe and along both American coasts. We'd bought *Blackwing,* our second cruising boat, three summers before. Now she was nicely broken in, sturdy and reliable, rigged with a self-tending jib and driven when necessary by a diesel auxiliary. She was beamy and heavy, built to go offshore and stay awhile. This was to be her first overnight passage offshore. Typically we sailed her within a fifty-mile radius of Jamestown, Rhode Island, where we lived then: to Cuttyhunk, Block Island, Nantucket, Stonington. These were frequently open-ocean passages, subject to what seemed like an impressive inventory of perils: storms, heavy seas, rain, patches of fog from time to time. But we'd depart in the morning, allow generous time to alter our course or destination to adjust to the weather, sail until late afternoon, provide a comfortable margin of daylight to find a mooring or drop anchor, watch the kids fish, have the Mount Gay poured before dusk, congratulate ourselves on our prudence and competence.

So we had decided soberly to let *Blackwing* convey us in measured stages from Jamestown to Penobscot Bay. First night at Cuttyhunk, second night at Wings Neck, riding the dawn tide east through the Cape Cod Canal followed by a nice downwind sail to Race Point. The final leg would be the new experience: sailing twenty-plus hours out of sight of land with virtually no seamarks, aiming for Monhegan, a big bold island with a lighthouse.

Assuming a clear night to let the full moon shine down its nighttime consolation, our enterprise nevertheless presented for us challenges of stamina and navigational sagacity. Priscilla—bearing full-time duties as cook, lookout, and general counsel—would give limited service at the helm. My sons could each keep a steady course, but they were kids: Nicholas was just shy of fourteen, Justin was eleven. Holding a precise course across the Gulf of Maine was no petty imperative. The currents swirl erratically, and given poor visibility an on-the-button landfall would be a matter of blind hazard. This dilemma kept circumspect sailors far from Maine. Its chief topographical attraction—rock-strewn coasts and myriad islands—makes close-to-shore sailing a grim option. Sailing Down East once upon a time separated lambs from wolves. The advent of affordable electronic navigational instruments teased the lambs forth, and here we were, bubbling "downhill" as sailors in those waters say of our course before the wind.

The state of electronic navigation in 1982 was transitional. Global positioning system (GPS) receivers, today almost as ubiquitous as the compass, were still a glimmer in the Pentagon's eye. Radar was big, clumsy, ruinously expensive, and unsuited to small sailboats. Prudent mariners who had experience sailing offshore in Maine were equipping themselves with Loran. This device, using land-based signals to triangulate positions, was tricky to tune and use, and it cost a pretty penny back then, maybe two thousand dollars. We must have spent half that sum on the cases of wine now being shaken to ruin stowed in our bilge. Still, I felt good vibes, the kind I'd once felt kicking the bald rear tire of a used street-racing Norton motorcycle and telling the salesman that I had a hunch the bike (dripping oil and festooned with lightning-bolt decals) had been fastidiously cared for, so didn't he agree I was wise to buy it? Besides, I was going to use a radio direction finder (RDF), a device that was basically a little radio turned this way and that to locate the null—or dead spot—on a radio transmitter signaling at known intervals from a known position. In our case this position was a tower atop Monhegan Island. Theoretically, one could sail along the path of this radio beam to its source. Aircraft had used RDF for many years. I had practiced in daylight with an evolved version of the instrument—a silent radio shaped like a pistol and with a compass for a sight—and I was satisfied with the approximate accuracy of the outcome. Nothing was perfect, and, as experienced sailors never tired of repeating, electronics were meant to be used as backups. A far-sighted offshore mariner navigated by visual reference and DR, dead reckoning, defined by one dictionary as "predictive calculation based on inference," defined by seafaring folk wisdom as "dead wrong."

After sunset I went below to catch a couple of hours of sleep, leaving Nicholas at the helm. I could feel the steady waves lift our transom and slew us a bit windward and feel him correct in the deliberate manner—nothing panicked or forced—of someone who knows what he is doing. Justin was in the cockpit with him, looking around for traffic. Their voices were low and steady, intimate. Priscilla was below, reading by the light of a kerosene lamp, as I listened to the weather radio. The Maine coastal forecast was summer-generic: wind southwest ten to twelve knots, with a chance of fog. This hard chance was forecast in a bored, matter-of-fact voice. In the twenty-first century marine forecasts are delivered by computer-generated voices,* but in

* The illusory "Paul," cobbled together from ones and zeroes, sounded like a Swede. Swedes objected, scoffed that he sounded like a Norwegian. Norwegians said he sounded like a guy from Minnesota. He was replaced by "Donna" and "Craig." Donna sounds way cooler than Craig, who seems to hail from Allentown, Pennsylvania.

1982 the dispassionate voice we heard was enough to chill me in my bunk. I poked my head through the companionway hatch to remind the boys that if the fog came, to wake me right away. The moon was dimmed by a screen of thin clouds, but I could see it. Went below; lay down; closed my eyes. Was gone.

Nicholas was talking. "It's here."

He sounded grim. It sure was there. My sleeping bag was heavy with it. My glasses were wet. I had no right to be surprised. Just before I went below I'd wiped moisture from the compass dome and cowl, and when I'd spoken to my boys in the cockpit I'd seen my breath. That had been more than two hours ago. Now Priscilla was sleeping.

"Did you see other boats?"

Justin said it had just happened. Not there and then there, moon blinking off like a burned-out bulb.

"But before it happened, did you see anything?" I willed my voice to hold steady. It was 3:35, and we were approaching the Portland shipping lanes. With any luck we would spot the big light on Monhegan in a few hours. Now I couldn't see the top of our mast, the bowsprit, anything out there that wasn't within touching distance. Like the Beaufort Scale used to grade winds systematically, meteorologists convey specific qualities by what sound to be loosely descriptive words:

"fog" occurs when horizontal visibility is reduced to less than two-thirds of a mile and "heavy fog" when it declines to a quarter-mile. This was past heavy. "Dense," you might call it, "thick o' fog." To describe the experience of this degree of fog at night, Roger Duncan—co-author of *The Cruising Guide to the New England Coast,* an East Boothbay citizen, and author of the authoritative *Sailing in the Fog*—abandons the language of exact measure and declares "you might as well have your head in a bag." *Sailing in the Fog* wasn't published until 1986, so how could we have known four years earlier Duncan's advice: "No one who goes to sea for pleasure would sail a boat among the ledges and islands of a broken coast at night in the fog. Anchor. Stay where you are."

I asked my sons again to tell me the last sights they had seen. They agreed that they'd noticed a set of fast-moving lights to seaward, heading across our bow. Pretty far ahead.

"How far?"

They couldn't say, they said. It was tricky to judge light at night, whether it was far off and bright or dim and near.

"Any other shipping?"

"Something on our course, coming up astern. A sailboat, maybe. I don't think it's moving faster than we are."

But we weren't moving. We might as well have been anchored. We were becalmed, rolling gently in the oily seas. The sails dripped dew; the boys dropped and furled them. We were "off-soundings," in water too deep to measure. That was good, I guessed. I fired up the faithful Yanmar diesel, never a missed beat these three years. Breathing felt difficult, as though a barber were holding a damp towel to my nose and mouth while I waited for a tanker to crawl into our cockpit. I posted Nick at the bowsprit, resumed forty-five degrees, smelled coffee cooking. Priscilla was looking through the hatch at the sky, ahead, astern at me.

"Priscilla ..." I began.

"Just keep your head," she said.

FOG IS: A METAPHOR. A BANK. A BLANKET THAT MAKES you shiver. Wet blanket. A wall. It's a bitch, a son of a bitch, everywhere in the universe (till it scoots away as slippery as it came, "scaling it up," as sailors say). It's a scare, a horror, can blind you to the ledge that will grind your keel and tear your rudder out, stonehearted, a stone killer. It's cunning and reckless, a damned freak, a dirty trick. It's ugly or beautiful, depending on whether you're a navigator or an aesthetician. Jack the Ripper used high humidity to cloak his bloodthirsty prowlings; J. M. W. Turner found filtered loveliness in vapor, steam, and what came to be called smog, the coal-fired, green-ish-yellowish-orangish-brownish infernal fog Dickens saw as "soft black drizzle." Edward Bullough, a Cambridge don, chose fog at sea to illustrate his influential theory of "psychical distance," adumbrated in 1912 in the *British Journal of Psychology:*

> *A short illustration will explain what is meant by "Psychical Distance." Imagine a fog at sea: for most people it is an experience of acute unpleasantness. Apart from the physical annoyance and remoter forms of discomfort such as delays, it is apt to produce feelings of peculiar anxiety, fears of invisible dangers, strains of watching and listening for distant and unlocalized signals. The listless movements of the ship and her warning calls soon tell upon the nerves of the passengers; and that special, expectant, tacit anxiety and nervousness, always associated with this experience, make a fog the dreaded terror of the sea (all the more terrifying because of its very silence and gentleness) for the expert seafarer no less than for the ignorant landsman.*
>
> *Nevertheless, a fog at sea can be a source of intense relish and enjoyment. Abstract from the experience of the sea fog, for the moment, its danger and practical unpleasantness.... Direct the attention to the features*

"objectively" constituting the phenomenon—the veil surrounding you with an opaqueness as of transparent milk, blurring the outline of things and distorting their shapes into weird grotesqueness; observe the carrying-power of the air, producing the impression as if you could touch some far-off siren by merely putting out your hand and letting it lose itself behind that white wall; note the curious creamy smoothness of the water, hypocritically denying as it were any suggestion of danger; and, above all, the strange solitude and remoteness from the world, as it can be found only on the highest mountain tops; and the experience may acquire, in its uncanny mingling of repose and terror, a flavor of such concentrated poignancy and delight as to contrast sharply with the blind and distempered anxiety of its other aspects. This contrast, often emerging with startling suddenness, is like a momentary switching on of some new current, or the passing ray of a brighter light, illuminating the outlook upon perhaps the most ordinary and familiar physical objects—an impression which we experience sometimes in instants of direct extremity, when our practical interest snaps like a wire from sheer overtension, and we watch the consummation of some impending catastrophe with the marveling unconcern of a mere spectator.

Now, writing this, I'm moved by the recollection of "curious creamy smoothness." Then, afloat in it, I was utterly the creature of "peculiar anxiety," exhausted and demoralized by "fears of invisible dangers."

Fog, we learn in the ninth-grade English class introducing us to metaphor, "comes on little cat feet." But we also learn in science class that fog is not a mystery. Just a low cloud is all, a cloud that touches land, sticks to water. The wind that had been shoving us along came from the southwest, no surprise, indeed the prevailing summer wind in those parts. The south part made the air warm; passing over the Gulf Stream made it warmer still, and humid. High humidity brought a high dew point, the temperature at which the air could not hold moisture latent. As the sun dropped and the moist, warm air collided with the cold water of the Gulf of Maine, churned by tidal action, that dew point was reached: Bingo. Just a humdrum atmospheric phenomenon in the neighborhood of the fog factories of the Bay of Fundy and the Labrador Current, more common than sunshine. We felt as though we'd been kidnapped. Oh, how I had counted on the Monhegan Island light! But the light could have been fixed to my damned bowsprit and I wouldn't have seen it. The decks were greased with wet and the gray swells were dirty. The air was like sour milk, dreadful yellow. The rigging, dripping morosely, brooded like gallows. I blew a foghorn with requisite regularity, and the dense, wet dark swallowed the doleful noise.

The night it ended I composed a log:

> *With Justin in the bow blowing a pitiful warning, with Nicholas below trying to recover from the night, with Priscilla deep in Duncan and Ware's* Cruising Guide to the New England Coast, *day breaks. Day breaks my heart. Black obscurity gives way to pearly obscurity. Portland marine weather promises a great day ashore, sunny and hot, good beach day, maybe a little hazy. Oh, by the way, offshore? Fog.*
>
> *Priscilla doesn't say, "How did you get us into this?" But how can I fail to know what she's thinking as she reads Roger F. Duncan and John P. Ware, whose celebration of the water we now blindly bob upon bristles with warning labels of treacherous tides, rocky shoals, evil weather, fog?*
>
> *Priscilla reads aloud from the humid pages something she thinks I might need to know: "The on-shore tide set from Portsmouth onward is a major navigation hazard. In spite of the fact that we make a major compensation for this effect we almost always fall inside of the anticipated landfall....*
>
> *"Does that bear on us?" Priscilla asks.*
>
> *I nod, shake my head. Confess, "I don't know."*

Because the tide sets in an irregular circular motion along the course we have sailed, I haven't the least notion where I am, not the foggiest, which is why this log is all description and no exposition. No facts to transcribe, just "beats me" and "dunno" and "huh?" As I will learn, at the helm I have indulged a known fog-bound sucker's bias, always slightly favoring east over west, the sea over the coast, overcorrecting the helm when Blackwing *swings to port, under correcting when she veers to starboard. The good news: I (probably) won't run us up on a rocky beach in Muscongus Bay; the bad news: Between us and Portugal are few bells, horns, whistles.*

At ten o'clock, our ETA for Monhegan, the diesel coughs, sputters. Nick's at the helm; I shout at him, assume he's adjusted the throttle; he hasn't. My irritated cry provokes alarm in the people I've brought here to make happy. I feel sorry for myself; I'm ashamed; I'm scared.

I'd been in fog before, fog as thick as this. I'd run buoy to buoy from Pulpit Harbor on North Haven into Camden. That was five years before, and when I'd missed a mark, I'd known enough to motor the boundaries of a square, shutting off the engine to listen, and I'd found my way. It had been a strain, of course, cramping the neck muscles, all that tensing to hear, that fierce concentration on the compass, but I had known where I was when the world went blind and the whistling buoy I sought was four miles distant, halfway to Camden. Distance multiplies the effect of error, but earlier this year we'd been swallowed by fog running from Block Island to Newport, and I hadn't panicked, just held on course fourteen miles for the Texas Tower, and there it was, its monster spider legs rising from the sea, on the button: *There!* That wasn't so hard, was it?

This was different. I tried to find Monhegan with the laughable RDF. The null suggested it was abeam, either port or starboard. Gee, thanks. The weather radio suggested a likely possibility of thunderstorms, and we prayed for them, to blow the fog away, part the veil for even an instant. A teasing zephyr astern drifted diesel exhaust at us.

We didn't speak. We listened. I dared not shut off the engine. I now believed so powerfully in entropy—in general disintegration and systematic failure, in bad luck—that I dared not alter anything: course, throttle, helmsman. We motored forward, forty-five degrees. Time had hung up. None of us had any sense of its duration. When the engine coughed (was even that reliable thumper preparing to stab me in the back?), I dumped into the tank our last jerrican of diesel, and I worried silently that we might soon run out of fuel. How could that be? Hadn't I prepared? Done the math? I tried to do the math now in my head and it never came out the same twice. We were all seeing coronas, occasional flashes of light around us. Samuel Eliot Morison has written about the persistence of mist-shawled mystery along this coast, its sailors seeing "fantastic figures in a lifting fog, [imagining] the towers and battlements of a shimmering dream-city; and someone who knows the story will sing out, 'Norumbega!'" The strobing phenomenon that day was sometimes a comfort—was the sun about to break through?—and more often a terror: What was *that?* These items we did not see: black cans or red nuns, birds, lobster pots, seals, boats, any way out of our fix. Now and then we imagined we heard a booming sound. We were listening for anything: a foghorn, a gull crying, a ship's bell, a ship's engine, surf breaking on rocks, something.

I can recall my fear in its shaming detail all these decades later. Truth is, of course, that the terror was mostly unfounded. We had a VHF marine radio aboard, and trailed behind us a seaworthy rubber dinghy powered by an outboard. It was improbable, with my family scrutinizing what there was of a horizon, that we'd hit anything. That was the problem: There appeared to be nothing around to hit. And even if there were, our speed was four knots. We weren't mountain climbers trying to get off the summit in a whiteout, but I was near frozen with anxiety and dread, and decades later, I came upon a piece of writing that suggested the elevator-falling quality of this panic, aggravated by the added dimension of altitude.

In James Salter's memoir *Burning the Days,* he tells of training as a pilot at the end of World War II. One May evening he was sent with others in his squadron on a navigation flight to Pennsylvania, from West Point to Scranton to Reading and home. They left while it was still light and soon were separated from one another. The information they had received about the direction and velocity of winds aloft had been inaccurate, and as the sun dropped and Salter flew west at an airspeed of 160 miles per hour, with "no one to see or talk to, the wind, unsuspected, was shifting us slowly, like sand." In common with seventeen-year-old drivers and with sailors like myself, pilots at Salter's level don't think about what they don't know, because they don't know they don't know it. Call it cockiness or call it blissful ignorance, it is dangerous. "Flying," Salter writes, "like most things of consequence, is method. Though I did not know it then, I was behaving improperly." He had failed to pay close enough attention to certain anomalies he might have noticed about the ground unspooling below, and he was unused to flying at night, "a different world" in the dark. "The instruments become harder to read, details disappear from the map." Then, as night cooled the Earth, a scrim of mist obscured the lights below. Salter, attempting to navigate by the same RDF system that I was using thirty-five years later in Maine, tuned and adjusted the volume to find a clear signal from Reading, Pennsylvania. No matter what course he flew, the signal grew weaker. Now he was watching the clock, and his fuel gauges. "Something was wrong, something serious: the signal didn't change. I was lost, not only literally but in relation to reality." Now panic attacked:

> *I turned northeast, the general direction of home. I had been scribbling illegibly on the page of memory, which way I had gone and for how long. I now had no idea where I was.... There was a terrible temptation to abandon everything, to give up, as with a hopeless puzzle.... I had the greatest difficulty not praying and finally I did, flying in the noisy darkness, desperate for the sight of a city or anything that would give me my position.*

Salter found in his map case a booklet, "What to Do if Lost," which he tried to read by flashlight. A half dozen steps were listed, to be performed in sequence. Some he had already tried, he thought, and in the dark, running out of fuel, he lost faith in the procedure. This was not bobbing on a gray ocean. This *would* end sooner than later. And it did, with Salter crash-landing on a field and onto the front porch of a house in Great, Massachusetts.*

PRISCILLA HEARD SOMETHING FIRST. THEN I IMAGINED I heard something and throttled back. We all cupped our ears, turning this way and that. Listening, Priscilla held her finger to her lips. Then we all heard it, a low moan, like the complaint of someone left alone with a belly-ache. The resigned lament would come and go. For an hour we sought it, steering box courses as I tried for a change to follow some conventional navigational routine. This required discipline, or ignorance: Often the course I was running three minutes to each leg would seem to take us away from the breathy warning signal, or perhaps this was the effect of a slight wind shift, or of the buoy (if that's what it was) ceasing to rock in those flat seas, or of an object—an oil tanker, let's imagine—coming between the buoy and us, or ... who knew? Then it

* "Fog Kills Songbirds in Bay of Fundy," the Canadian Broadcasting Corporation recently reported. Fishermen tell of sea birds falling onto their decks from the sky; the birds—lost in fog—become wet and heavy, too cold and miserable to fly.

appeared and once we saw it, we couldn't imagine not having seen it. Reason told me that the whistle marked "SL" had not been placed to tell us where we were but to mark a hazard. Nick urged me to creep up on it and I did, because I was stalking the whistle, feared I'd spook it. But it stayed put, fifty feet off, anchored. I envied it. Now it groaned frankly, excessively.

Justin took the helm and circled the mark while I went below to hail the Coast Guard on Channel 16. My voice did not reassure me. I had once had a bad stutter, and it had come back. Was there an "SL," black and white, n-n-n-n-ear Mon-hee-hee-hah-heh-huh-hegan?

That was a negative, skipper. We were circling a buoy on the Seal Ledges, a little east of Large Green Island, fourteen nautical miles east-northeast of Monhegan, which we had missed by a mile, exactly. We were in *bad* water, with a foot between our keel and a kelpy rock slab, and the Coast Guard suggested we get ourselves out of there, "with all due haste," to Matinicus Island, three miles southeast. Looking back, I guess we should have felt rescued. But our least desired course that afternoon was a course to seaward that would leave behind us the one thing we knew, yonder whining whistle. The weather radio was undecided between thunderstorms and dense fog, growing denser. We went for Matinicus and its little sister a bit seaward—Ragged—trying to pick up a red nun buoy on the Foster Ledges, R10, 155 degrees, a mile and eight-tenths, twenty minutes or so distant. No bells or whistles enhanced R10, and we missed it; it could have been thirty feet from us and we'd have missed it. We should have been near Matinicus. Priscilla was reading: "The region should be approached with caution. There are no really snug harbors ... unmarked dangers are frequent, and tides are swift. In fog or storm the careless or inexperienced can get into real trouble."

Justin was on the bowsprit, shouting, "Look at those thunderclouds!"

I looked up, saw black, smelled Christmas. Pines on a cliff, trailing beards of gray mist. And then we were among rocks, and a rocky beach materialized yards ahead. I swung the wheel over while Nick yelled directions, and we *didn't* grind out on a ledge or tear open the hull, or even stub our toe. It was high tide.

We anchored. I got on the radio: "Anybody on Ragged Island or Matinicus. Anybody. Please come back, please. This is *Blackwing*. I am looking at a rocky beach on the west side of one of your islands. We are tired. And lost. I repeat [sic], we are frightened. Please come back."

And there came a lobsterman, clear-voiced. Said he was pulling pots, he had us on his radar, would drop by in a jiffy, lead us into Criehaven, the harbor on Ragged. He had an extra mooring, he said, we could use it. Drink a cup of coffee, he suggested. Take it easy. Welcome to Maine, he said.

I could have wept. Asked again—"Do you sail?"—I would have responded, "Sort of, maybe, not really." Did mister manly man resent how his woman and sons already felt about the savior with radar, and sense enough to find his way to a safe haven? I did not. My he-manliness, poor pathetic thing, was back there in the Portland shipping lanes, or where I'd lost my wits somewhere near Monhegan, where I'd gone plumb numb.

When the lobsterman came alongside and saw my hands shaking, he suggested, seeing how thick o' fog it was, that he *tow* us in. That seemed to me the brightest idea anyone ever had. He towed, disappeared into the murk as the line went taut; I pretended to steer, and the boys and Priscilla went below to talk about something. Criehaven's a snug harbor, and when we entered I knew from the chart that we passed a breakwater not twenty-five feet to starboard. We never saw it. And till the fog lifted we never saw land from *Blackwing*.

We hung on a mooring in Criehaven two days, two nights. That first night it cleared, and we saw the Northern Lights. Snug below, I listened to Nick on the forward deck explain with the timeworn patience of an older brother that the flashes were in fact World War III.

Justin, evidently undeceived, said, "I'm glad we're here."

"Amen," Priscilla said from the cockpit.

Next morning: fog. We stayed put. If the fog hadn't lifted, we'd still be there, believe me. Back then, it was a common idiom of cruising guides to warn that a Maine fog could keep you so long anchored in one place that you'd ground on your own beer cans before you'd dare move. But the fog did lift, as it does. And way short of disaster it could have been worse. Roger Duncan has described sailing in a Penobscot Bay fog so thick that the Vinalhaven ferry coming in from Rockland with radar couldn't find her slip. As for him:

> We underestimated the tide, mistook one headland we had never seen for another equally unfamiliar, got into a nest of half-tide rocks, bounced off one, stuck on another, but fortunately sailed her clear. We anchored, guessed, speculated, blundered about from island to island for three hours, went ashore and asked a party of clam diggers where we were, and at length made a safe harbor in the falling dark. Better we had not tried it.

So now? I feel less and less like a fool, which is striking evidence of foolishness. More and more it has seemed to be a good idea to venture offshore, so we do. But never with Monhegan as a destination. Let's call it a bad vibe coming from Monhegan, a really weak signal.

ANCHORED: RAGGED ISLAND

At dawn the dripping hatch above our bunk told all we needed to know. To sink my account even deeper in Roger F. Duncan's debt, here's his perfectly condensed description of our situation, fog dew drumming softly on the deck in a melancholy, irregular rhythm, the muffled "complaint of gulls standing on their weir stakes waiting for something good to happen." But good was happening, the quickening experience of waking up in a place you'd never planned to find yourself. Pleasures can come as an outcome of having a trip diverted by weather: A flight meant for Barcelona is redirected to Lisbon, a stop in Reykjavik is forced owing to the inclemency of Gander. We had planned our Maine cruise with compulsive care, but this Ragged Island I had never heard of. I knew of another Ragged Island, in

Casco Bay, not far from Cundy Harbor, where Edna St. Vincent Millay had lived.

There are so many islands along the Maine coast— one for every day of the year in Casco Bay alone—that an outcropping here often winds up with the same name as another over yonder: There are six Greens, a pair of Swans, a couple of Calfs and Cows (and a West Brown Cow), and Moose and Mouses and Minks and Otters and Porcupines and eight Rams and nine Hogs and thirteen Sheep. (Some of these Sheep Islands are named for their rough likeness to the beast, but most are descriptive of patches of grazing land safe from predators.) Of Eagles there are three (in Penobscot Bay, Casco Bay, and Blue Hill Bay) and twice that number of Crows. A few Stones and Turnips, a couple of Potatoes. There are half a dozen Burnt Islands, a Burnt Coat Island, and a Burnt Coat Harbor. Maine has seven Harbor Islands, christened no doubt in hasty gratitude by casual explorers who had noticed while at anchor in some safe haven worth remembering a nearby island. Maine has three Crotch Islands and Long Islands aplenty; there's a Bailey Island and Baileys Mistake and Despair Island. The only Thief Island is kept under control by nearby High Sheriff. The Hypocrites and The Cuckholds have tales to tell. There's a pair of Folly Islands, telling a pair of old stories. Why the need for a

Smuttynose Island at the Isle of Shoals and another near Monhegan? In *The Folklore of Maine,* Horace P. Bec tells of a pair of small outcroppings near Vinalhaven, Murder and Bury, on one of which a family of settlers were done in by Indians and on the other—"where the digging was easier"—they were buried. Down east near Beals Island—author Louise Rich explains that the U.S. Board on Geographical Names disfavors the use of apostrophes, excepting Penobscot Bay's Swan's Island—Virgin's Breast Ledge and The Lecherous Priest have disappeared from recent charts. Thrumcap is so apt a name—referring to the conical cap of tufty furlike wool worn by sailors—that there had to be two. Bar Islands abound, and there are Bares (as well as Bears). Near Islesboro is a Tumbledown Dick. There are Littles and Bigs side-by-side and far apart, ditto Highs and a Lower. There's a Bush Island and a Twobush Island in Muscongus Bay and a Two Bush Island in Merchant Row. Isle au Haut, named for its height by the French explorer Samuel de Champlain, was for a time corrupted on British and American charts to Aisle O'Holt, and returned now to its original appellation is fancifully pronounced a variety of ways, including EEL-ee o A-leee. The pronunciation of Mount Desert— named by Champlain Mont Desert for its barren appearance—requires a summer resident with the authority of Samuel Eliot Morison to sort out. In his wry and casual little book, *The Story of Mount Desert Island,* Morison settles the matter. "We may grapple with the problem … whether we should follow what many people call the 'Sahara School' and accent the penult, pronouncing it 'Mount DEZ-ert,' or what opponents call the 'Ice Cream and Cake School,' pronouncing it 'Mount DEZ-ERT' with accent on the last syllable…. At the time of writing [1961] the penult accenters are much in a minority."

The descriptive impulse is a culture-specific and nature-contingent motive in the naming of islands: Yesterday's Burnt might be today's Green, or vice versa, and Two Bush has a way of becoming One Bush or Hundred Bush. An island namer in the New Meadows River threw in the towel and gave to three islands a single name: Three Islands. Within sight of our anchorage in Criehaven was a Matinicus Island and a Matinicus Rock. Except for Matinicus Rock (home to a thriving colony of puffins), the farthest offshore inhabited land belonging to the United States is Criehaven's Ragged Island. Its current name was modified by the priggishness of geodetic service chartmakers from its original title, Ragged Arse. Some students of Maine's place-names have decided that this earlier designation was a corruption of the Indians' designation, Racketash, or perhaps Raggertusk. Horace P. Bec alludes to its naughty name as descriptive of Ragged's erstwhile topography and flora: a "bold front ... with a broken and battered backside." On the same page, Bec tells a more vivid story of the island's earliest English name, on a chart issued in 1790, Cold Arse: "South and a little east of Matinicus lies a miserable, cucumber-shaped rock pile with only a few trees and a tiny, exposed, foul harbor, Criehaven, that now bears the name of Ragged Island. We need no story," Bec speculates, "to tell us that some poor fisherman was marooned there during a cold winter's night in the eighteenth century. We know how he thrashed up and down in a vain attempt to keep warm. We know the dark thoughts he had for company in his arduous vigil and we know, too, that he was rescued" and gave the site of his misery its demeaning name. (Residents of Ragged Island know it as Criehaven; neighbors on Matinicus call it Ragged Arse, or Raggedy Ass.)

Rescue and hospitality are recurring motifs in the stories of this last stop before the edge-of-the-world. Like those rulers of Homer's *Odyssey* who welcome and feed strangers, the seasonal inhabitants of Criehaven take care of wanderers. The overseers of those waters are mostly lobstermen, a dozen or so, who spend spring to fall out there hauling an abundant harvest from the deep waters, returning to the mainland and their families on weekends and for the winter, when cruel gales punish the outlying islands. You'd think that people who had found Maine's other coastal outposts too crowded for comfort would be suspicious of aliens, reflexively resentful. Mainers label anyone not native to their place "from away," and how much farther away could we have been from, a crew led by a captain blubbering (on a still day and floating free on still water), *help help, we're lost.*

Rescue is an old tradition in remote and severe places. Land's End at the tip of Cornwall was the site of a legendary lifesaving station whose Samaritans routinely rescued sailors lost or battered or going down in the English Channel. Criehaven was a last-chance kind of place even before the first mainland colonists arrived at Popham in 1607. It was a thriving fishing outpost as early as the sixteenth century and maybe before then. There are unsubstantiated theories that Vikings sailed Maine's bays and a legend that the Phoenicians found their way there even earlier. If they did, they must have lost themselves in fog, or been beaten up by a gale, and woe to them if they couldn't raise Criehaven on Channel 16. Nearer in time, in 1939, Alfred F. Loomis, a celebrated chronicler of his exploits as an ocean racer and cruiser, wrote *Ranging the Maine Coast.* It gives the account of the voyage of his 32-foot cutter *Hotspur* from Kittery at the New Hampshire border to West Quoddy Head, the perversely named location of America's easternmost frontier with Canada. (It's a point-of-view thing.) Loomis gives over a few pages to his expedition to Criehaven with his crewmate Paul Wisner. Contemplating the tricky waters near Green Island and Deadman Ledge, Loomis "squared away for Ragged Arse Island, where Paul had a debt of gratitude to pay." It seems that a year earlier, en route from Nova Scotia to Buzzards Bay, Wisner and his brother Jack "had become embroiled in a northeaster which gave them sufficient opportunity to reflect on the mitigating benefits of life insurance." They managed to get lost, confusing the island they were seeking (Metinic) for one they were avoiding (Matinicus). Armed with teeth, Matinicus was showing them through surf breaking on its ledges when they were discovered by a fisherman from Criehaven, who guided them into that harbor where they were "dried out and rendered comfortable during the ensuing days that the northeaster raged."

Like all island dwellers, Criehaven's year-rounders were alert to the lucky breaks of outsiders' unlucky breakups at sea, flotsam driven by the caprice of wind and tide to their shores. Dorothy Simpson, author of *The Island's True Child,* an account of her demanding childhood and early life as a lobsterman's daughter on Ragged Island from 1911 till World War II, tells of her community's fevered gathering of planks, including varnished pine and hardwood—the detritus of a wooden ship crushed by a winter storm. Everyone, grandmas and toddlers, grabbed pieces of the treasure. In an economy that obliged children to scour beaches for bits of driftwood to fire the wood stoves, such a bonanza might make islanders eager to enjoy the fruits of strangers' mishaps at sea. But there are instances aplenty of the geniality of Ragged Island's citizens. In the November 1995 *Down East* magazine is a story by Steve Waterman, an ex-Navy Seal, diver, and lobsterman from South Thomaston who, the previous November, had rescued a single-engine plane, a Lake Aircraft amphibian, that went down thirty-six miles offshore after flying from England to Maine by way of Newfoundland. The pilot had been lifted from some mighty chilly water by the Coast Guard, a rescue Waterman picked up on his police scanner. He decided to salvage the airplane, and the story of his enterprise and unlikely success came complete with a photo of *Lake Renegade* #N26LA hauling at its mooring in Criehaven harbor after a three-day winter blow that kept Waterman and his friend hostage in the fishing camp of one Buzzy, a Ragged Islander. It's a good story, a cautionary tale of how quickly and awfully prospects can deteriorate offshore. Not only did Waterman have to seek refuge in Criehaven at night in a sleet storm, the tug sent out by an insurance company representing the interests of the airplane's owner managed to foul its propeller in a ground line that stretches from shore to shore, serving to secure the harbor's moorings (the bottom is slippery, hard sand and granite).

Many a warning's been issued in cruising guides about that ground line, and the three-foot ledge smack in the middle of Criehaven's field of moorings. Such ground lines—communal chains stretched across the harbor floor—are customary in some of the offshore islands favored by fishermen. It is ill advised, if not impossible, to anchor at Monhegan owing to the tangle of chains crisscrossing its harbor, and neighboring Matinicus Island is notorious for its inhospitality to cruisers, owing in part to limited anchor room. *The Cruising Guide to the New England Coast* warns sailors against hooking up to absent fishermen's moorings: "Keep off them unless you get permission, for a seiner returning at 4 a.m. after a night's work to find a yachtsman asleep on his mooring can be a bit surly."

Islands are fragile by their nature, and remote islands are especially provisional. A small patch of terra firma bounded by water allows little tolerance for bad luck: natural calamity, ill health, a crashing market in fish or lobsters, social friction. For a restricted and insular population the consequence of error or ill will is aggravated. The strain of being a good neighbor in such a tight space is acute, and the damage done by a careless or selfish outsider (mainlanders as well as those "from away") is magnified. A few visits from sailors who demand fuel and water from islanders who haven't much of either and who never invited the visitors in the first place, a laissez-faire approach to island property—walking across a yard, picking someone's blueberries—can ramify to form a generalized prejudice among the hosts. And the amplification of grievances echoes, so that certain islands become legendary among outsiders for the biliousness of its inhabitants. A story is told of a Matinicus lobsterman who suspected an off-islander of cutting his traps, either from malice or territorial belligerence. Matinicus has a modest airstrip and the lobsterman had access to an airplane. He flew over his enemy's lobster boat and dropped on it a boulder the size of an unsheared sheep; the offending vessel sank.

But to give Ragged Island's lobstermen their due in comparative bellicosity, they reserve an acute animus against Matinicus Island's fleet and its inevitable overlapping of their sea floor. In the 1950s, as narrated by Colin Woodard in his *Lobster Coast,* "hundreds of traps were destroyed" in these waters, "fishing shacks were burned to the ground and a few fishermen shot. 'My

Lord, those guys on Criehaven were shooting over the heads of any people from outside their island who tried to put traps there,' recalls ... Maine's fisheries commissioner at the time. 'Finally I had one of my wardens come back telling me he had to get way down in his boat because the bullets were coming so close to his windshield.... They played rough in those days.'" As recently as 1999 a melee broke out at the town dock among Criehaven lobstermen, one of whom had been ostracized as a maverick for setting as many traps as he pleased, wherever he pleased, in waters' whose territories were understood to be marked by unwritten but sacred agreements. The dispute had been on a low boil for a couple of years until the offender was suspected of having made obscene drawings on the trap buoys of a neighbor. "A bunch of the old boys decided to teach him a lesson, and he stood up to them," in the words of the outlaw's attorney, whose client was charged with aggravated assault. The Maine Supreme Court, in a finding of fact, reported that "a verbal confrontation ensued with, according to the record, a number of salty Down East expressions being exchanged." The old boys were armed with pitchforks, and the counterattacker came at the eldest of them with a gaff, a sharpened boat hook, and blood was shed.

Wooden Ball Island, a mile-long grassy rock a few miles east of Matinicus, supported a couple of inhabitants many years ago (more than can be claimed by nearby No Mans Land). The two men lived in uneasy amity until one somehow offended the other by leaving undone a chore. Umbrage ensued, followed by fisticuffs all through a moonlit night. The bout was scored no decision, and the following morning one of the erstwhile friends got in his rowboat and headed east, away from Matinicus, and the other got in *his* and rowed to Matinicus. I have a hunch he was the surly one.*

With the exception of the legendary Abbie Burgess—the daughter of the keeper from 1853 to 1861 of Matinicus Light, the station farthest offshore in American waters—the hired inhabitants were famously disenchanted with having been stranded on a surf-beaten puffin colony. Abbie's standing in the state's folklore is unsurpassed. She was fourteen when her father, invalid mother, and little sisters came to the Rock, lured there by a salary of fifty dollars per year. She trimmed and fueled the wicks, adjusted the optics, stood watch, raised chickens, nursed her mother. During a winter

*The feuds between residents of Ragged Island and Matinicus are exacerbated by a natural hostility given their proximity. Perhaps owing to the superior endurance of Matinicus as a year-round community, its citizens have been known to look down on their neighbors as self-destructive. In *Islands of the Mid-Maine Coast,* Charles and Carol McLane tell of a summer visitor on Matinicus who, "hearing gunfire one day on Criehaven, asked a [Matinicus native] what they were shooting over there and received the laconic reply, 'Each other.'"

storm in 1856, with supplies and medicine running low after the supply ship had unaccountably neglected to stop at Matinicus Light, Abbie's father left the Rock to journey twenty-five miles to Rockland. A northeast storm stranded him ashore, while it battered the lighthouse. Abbie twice saved her mother's life by moving her to higher ground. The following winter, while her father was again trapped ashore, a terrific gale battered Matinicus Rock, breaking waves over it and sweeping away the light keeper's house. The towers stood, damaged, and for almost a month Abbie attended to her family and even her five hens, rescuing four. She rationed food, went without sleep, and kept the light burning. In 1861 a new keeper, John Grant, was given this plum of a job by Abraham Lincoln, and Abbie married his son, Isaac, and for fourteen years she remained on the Rock, where four Grant children were born.

From 1827 until the light was automated the year following our unplanned visit, its succession of tenders failed to romanticize their service. A successful landing on the volcanic pile could be achieved only during flat calm or with good luck. Bill Caldwell, in *Lighthouses of Maine,* quotes an 1891 description by the government Light House Board of the procedure: The light keeper "effects a landing by steering his boat through the breakers on top of a wave so that it will land on the boat ways, where his assistants stand ready to receive him, and draw his boat up so far on the ways that a receding wave cannot carry it back to the sea." The light's purpose, to cast a signal at least nineteen miles and to sound a signal through fog, was compromised by the battering the lights took, and by poor light design. For a time Matinicus was to distinguish itself by showing two lights from two towers, but even at short ranges these appeared as a single illumination, confounding mariners. Then the Lighthouse Board specified a red signal, but this severely truncated the light's range. A fog bell was tried, but no one at sea could hear it.

The final string of exiles on the Rock—so-called stag-light keepers posted there by the Coast Guard—publicized their unhappiness, complaining to the rare visitor, writing letters of bitter regret and recrimination to the editors of such periodicals as the *Maine Coast Fisherman*. Louise Dickinson Rich, in her often rapturous and some-times sardonic *Coast of Maine* (1956), an "informal history and guide," catches the spirit of the Coast Guardsmen's dispatches: "pathetic letters ... telling how nice it was back in Minnesota, with the wheat fields blowing and one's best girl just down the road."

In the 1890s a lonely keeper, William Grant (son of Abbie and Isaac, born on the Rock), brought a cow to the island, having her ferried over from Matinicus

Island. Bill Caldwell quotes a journalist writing, after a visit to Matinicus light in 1897, for *Century Magazine*. Gustav Kebbe describes the cow, Daisy, "standing on that mass of barren rock, the only living thing in view, the wind furrowing up her hide. She would gaze out at the waste of wild waters with a driven, lonely look.... Often the cow looks over in the direction of Matinicus Island and moos pathetically.... She formerly found some companionship in a rabbit, with which she was accustomed to play at dusk, but the rabbit died."

It is little wonder the marooned were bitter. A fine nesting ground for puffins and petrels and terns and shearwaters and peregrine falcons, Matinicus Rock is a god-awful misery of granite cliffs and shingle, treeless, shrubless, grassless, and fuzzed with peat. In the winter, sea smoke as thick as fur made even the shore disappear from sight. Its keepers—their lungs stabbed by wind-driven frost—had to chip ice off the lens ninety feet up to keep the light visible. On calm summer days some intrepid Audubon Society "puffin-grubbers" tried to land to observe the appealingly clownish sea parrots catch fish (more than a dozen stuffed crosswise in their beaks), but the incessant swells rolling in unbroken across the Atlantic had a nasty way of swamping or capsizing their dinghies. Forty feet at its highest natural elevation, the Rock is hammered silly by winter gales, rolling ten-ton boulders around like marbles. Legend is that one solitary keeper hanged himself in the light tower. Horace Bec tells in *The Folklore of Maine* that his ghost was malevolent, creating "all kinds of mischief, breaking dishes and slamming doors, and making a general nuisance of itself, causing the light to snuff itself or the foghorn to fail to blow."

Neighboring Ragged Islanders, with much to resent, mostly treat strangers and themselves well. Our lobster-fishing hero, after he finished pulling pots the next day, directed us around the walking paths of his island, giving the equivalent of a letter of introduction: "If anyone looks at you funny, say you're visiting Tom." Tom's island, which he shared with commuters like himself based on the mainland, together with a few summer people who came from as far away as New Jersey, has the unapologetic starkness of Brittany. What grew in that fog-damped soil seemed indestructibly rooted. The walking paths wandering south a mile from Criehaven—through wildflowers and wild rose and wild strawberries, through gorse and heather and neglected apple orchards—were almost tentative, as incidental as animal tracks. The late afternoon light was filtered by brume, but from an overgrown meadow at the southern edge of Ragged we could see through our binoculars the spume of breakers hurling themselves against Matinicus Rock, a few miles to the southeast. The wind whispered and rustled stunted trees at the beach's edge; waves slapped against Brig Ledge and wheeling terns and guillemots quarreled.

We knew a bit about Ragged and Matinicus from the cruising guides we carried aboard *Blackwing,* but Tom had added details. The first Europeans who gathered in the outer islands came there to catch and dry and salt fish. John Smith sent fishing schooners on successful ventures to Ragged and Matinicus Islands from the Jamestown Colony in Virginia; the returning fishermen told of abundant stands of spruce on the Maine islands. The first settlers were Harriet and Robert ("King") Crie, newlyweds in 1848, immigrants from Matinicus Island. The Cries and their children and in-laws were industrious farmers and fishers, lumbermen and sawyers; they raised hay and grazed as many as three hundred sheep, and the place thrived. A two-masted black schooner, *Conqueror,* called regularly from Boston, bringing food, hardware, and a few luxuries heading Down East, loading up on lobsters on her way home. By the beginning of the twentieth century Criehaven was attracting a summer colony of writers and artists and layabout rusticators. There was regular mailboat service from Rockland, and Louise Rich tells that doctors were easily summoned by carrier pigeons bearing messages to the mainland. Louise Rich lived elsewhere, though Dorothy Simpson's baby brother died in part because of the delay in diagnosis and treatment caused by his father having to cross twenty-five miles of open ocean in a lobster smack to Rockland, and return with a doctor, who commanded that the sick child be taken to Rockland, where he died and from where his coffin was borne across twenty-five miles of open ocean to Criehaven. Ragged Island supported a school and a church. In 1937 there were twenty houses and fifty-five full-time residents; Criehaven had a gas dock and store and post office. In 1956, at the time when Rich wrote about it, Ragged Island had "simmered down into a comfortable and pleasant middle age." By 1990 the island was overrun with rabbits, someone's bad idea, which flourished without predators. In 1996, Hank and Jan Taft's *Cruising Guide to the Maine Coast* reported of "beautiful Ragged Island" that "there's no store, no school, no post office, hardly any way to get there." World War II did Ragged Island in: the Army carried away its last teacher, so the schoolhouse was closed. The children moved ashore to go to school and their mothers followed. With fewer customers on Criehaven, the storekeeper shut shop. Without addressees, the mailboat, lifeline to the island, quit coming. Finally the men came ashore.

Depending on who's counting and what they count, Maine has about three thousand islands. A hundred years ago, three hundred islands had year-round communities; today the number is fourteen. Ragged Island's social and economic decline was gradual but inexorable. It was the last island community in Maine to "go extinct." The Tafts quote George Putz, who wrote for *Island Journal* an essay about the phenomenon of desuetude: "Though island communities are elegant in their social orders, they are for the same reason more prone to reverses brought about by only one or two events. The death of an influential man, the loss of a mailboat, a teacher, a store, or a breakwater (breached by the infamous Groundhog Day storm of 1976, wiping out Criehaven's fleet and wharves) may have influence out of proportion to comparable events in mainland communities where more options are available." In 1982 we experienced a near ghost town. The 2000 census reports a "total population of zero."

SOME LAUNDRY SNAPPED ON A LINE BEHIND A FISHERMAN'S house. No kids played down on the waterfront, where we saw piles of nets and traps and coiled lines, the tools of the only business that continued to make economic sense so far offshore. Lobsters from those waters are prized as the tastiest in Maine. The water is so cold that they shed later, which is thought to keep their meat more tender. We put this reputation to the test when Tom quietly materialized behind us as we stood studying Criehaven's rickety wharves.

"Let's eat," he said. Then he fed the four of us half a dozen lobsters and tucked into the rum and canned peaches we brought ashore. He shared his house with his nephew, a shy kid from Tenants Harbor who served as Tom's sternman, hauling and baiting traps for a cut of the take. The house, directly on the harbor, was a two-story clapboard cape with a sagging front porch, long past hoping for a coat of paint. It was just the kind of place you might find for sale these days in the back of *Down East* or *Maine Boats and Harbors,* going for $350,000, say, with 350 feet of waterfront. The interior was airy, with two big bedrooms upstairs. Tom wasn't planning on weekend guests, because he went home to Rockland every weekend to visit his wife and kids. No running water, and the kitchen, with a propane stove and ice box, was a museum recording Maine's taste in linoleum during the forty years since World War II. The place was uncluttered and spotless, lit by kerosene lamps. He had a generator, but fuel for it was a challenge to transport, he said—a few minutes before he insisted that we take five gallons of diesel to make sure we had enough to get us to the mainland.

Before we returned to *Blackwing,* Tom told us a story that made me feel smart ... or at least lucky. The tale was from that line of legends that ascribes subhuman feck-lessness or superhuman wisdom to Mainers who take to the sea, especially touching on their powers to pick their way through fog to a desired destination. These people, proud of their fog, bristle at the suggestion that any place else in the world—the Aleutians, say, or Cape Disappointment off the mouth of the Columbia River—might be as gloomy. "Even the birds be walkin'," Tom had said of the conditions yesterday. To cruise the Maine coast is to hear tales of fog. The Boston-Bangor steamer *City of Bangor,* for instance, ran right up on Monhegan in 1902 and *then* heard, as from many leagues distant, the foghorn close enough to hit with a cat; passengers were hurled from their bunks but none injured, excepting an acrobatic trick bicycle rider from Michigan. Piloting back then, when many ships moved fast and on schedule carrying freight and passengers, was an art. Local knowl-edge was valued: A few captains cutting close to shore would whistle, time their echoes, and fix their positions accordingly. One captain was said to identify his place by the particular bleating of particular sheep. Of these sto-ries some are true. A sailor did ram a school bus in Muscongus Bay—it was on a ferry, with kids aboard, moored to a buoy in thick o' junk o' fog. The master of a steam yacht clanked full astern twenty feet from the front door of a colonial farm house—being transported in dense fog from Phippsburg to Beauchamp Point—in forty fathoms off Seguin Island. Some of the tales may be apocryphal—of fog so dense you could walk home on it; fog so dense you could hang your laundry on it; fog so dense you could hammer shingles to its walls. The estimable Marshall Dodge and Robert Bryan, the 1950s Yalies better known as "Bert and I," made a nice living and gave much pleasure telling in a Down East dialect of the misadventures of the captain and mate of the lobster boat *Bluebird*. These characters were forever grounding out in the fog, and on one memorable occasion they went high and dry on a whale. A staple of the lore that fed this comedy routine was the misapplication of that quality so prized by sailors, "local knowledge." Sailing through toothy waters in a windy pea-souper with all canvas flying, the anxious helmsman is under orders from his captain, napping below, to press on at top speed, every so often casting the lead line and bringing to the captain a sample of the bottom. At the business end of a lead weight secured to the heaving line was a gob of tallow, and the seafloor's mud or sand or grass would stick to it. If the bottom was granite, it came up clean. In fable, the captain so reliably knows the composition of the bottom of Maine waters that this peculiar sand of just this density alerts him to his exact position, one and one-sixth leagues sou'west by south of Mistake Island. The punch line to these tales of wonderment is routinely ironic. Examining the residue the captain shouts out, "Keep a sharp lookout, boys! Accordin' to my figgerin' we're ten yards alee of Seth Eaton's barn."

Tom's story was of a misadventure that had befallen the skipper and crew of a dragger from way up west in Gloucester. This happened some years before, but what brought the story to Tom's mind, he said, was that like us this crew was Monhegan-bound, and like us they got shut in by a pea-souper. Having given up on the light on Monhegan, they were listening for the whistle nearby. No whistle. Time passed, and finally they anchored. A couple of hours later, come dawn, a lobster boat appeared nearby. "Where are we at?' asked the Gloucestermen. Matinicus was where. On a ledge was where. They'd anchored over that ledge with a foot or so to spare at the high point of a full moon tide. A month later the moon filled again, the tide washed enough water over the ledges to float the dragger, and the fishermen dragged their asses home to Gloucester.

Time to weigh anchor.

CHILLY WELCOMES

Giovanni da Verrazzano, sailing under the flag of France, visited the coast of Maine in 1524. However much he may have admired the flora, fish, and vistas of the shore near Cape Small and Pemaquid Point, he disapproved of the natives. For their part, the Abnaki—having had previous experience of visitors "from away"—treated Verrazzano and his crew with scorn. Pierre Crignon's fabulation of glorious Norumbega fraudulently named Verrazzano as the explorer so impressed with the native inhabitants' docility and comeliness and goldsmithing skill. The facts of the encounter were otherwise: "Clothed in peltry of bear, lynx, 'sea wolves' and other beasts," the Indians shot arrows at the Europeans as they tried to land. Nevertheless, some primitive trade was conducted between the visitors and the visited, by the expedient of exchanging goods placed in baskets lowered from the headland cliff to the beach below. The Europeans, surrendering fish hooks and knives and receiving in return a few root vegetables, got the worst of the deal, a shame emphatically commemorated by the Abnaki, who "showed all signs of discourtesy and disdain, as was possible for any brute creature to invent, such as exhibiting their bare behinds and laughing immoderately." Verrazzano's contempt for the natives' rude disregard for European courtesy is recorded in Samuel Eliot Morison's *The European Discovery of America,* which reports as well that the celebrated explorer baptized the Maine coast Terre Onde di Mala Gente, Land of Bad People.

The Abnaki had their grievances against explorers, and I guess many lobstermen* have theirs against yachties. They dismiss sailing vessels as "blow boats," and blow boaters either amuse or aggravate them. As with Abnaki, lobstermen run the temperamental scale from tolerant to agitated, and local history—tales told and retold at the co-op down by the town wharf—retails the individual responses to the presence of many mariners with different priorities. The captain of a container ship

* People in Maine who fish—according to as celebrated and reliable an authority as Linda Greenlaw—refer to themselves, whichever their gender, as "fishermen" and "lobstermen."

or the high-speed ferry bound from Bar Harbor to Nova Scotia means to go in as straight a line as possible, and his cry is, "Look out, here I come, make way!" The new ferry *Cat,* a behemoth with thirty-eight-thousand horsepower running forty miles per hour on wave-piercing double hulls, has already mowed down a fishing boat in Yarmouth, Nova Scotia, killing her captain. Her huge wake comes out of nowhere, adrenaline-pumping indeed in the fog.

Right-of-way on the water seems at first glance to be a matter of common sense: Keep to the right is the basic rule. But maritime litigators make comfortable livings off the exceptions. A sailboat on starboard tack (with the wind blowing over its right rail and toward its left) has right-of-way over a sailboat on port tack. A sailboat not under engine power has right of way over a sailboat using the iron jib. A sailboat hard on the wind (sailing so close to the wind—or "pinched"—that it has limited maneuverability to windward) has right-of-way over a sailboat sailing off the wind. Sailboats have right-of-way over powerboats, *except* ... there are many fine-tuned *excepts,* most matters of fundamental common sense. Except when the motorboat is dragging nets, let's say, or the oil tanker requires two miles to stop its forward motion.

Surfing the net a few years ago, looking for chart updates to navigational hazards and marks in the area of Grand Manan Island, I bumped into this transcript of a radio communication between Canadian authorities and the bridge of a United States Navy ship approaching Newfoundland in limited visibility but with state-of-the-art radar on October 10, 1995. The transcript was released by our Chief of Naval Operations:

AMERICANS: Please divert your course fifteen degrees to the north to avoid a collision.

CANADIANS: Recommend you divert YOUR course fifteen degrees to the SOUTH to avoid a collision.

AMERICANS: This is the captain of a U.S. Navy ship. I say again, divert YOUR course.

CANADIANS: No. I say again, you divert YOUR course.

AMERICANS: THIS IS THE AIRCRAFT CARRIER U.S.S. *LINCOLN,* THE SECOND LARGEST SHIP IN THE UNITED STATES ATLANTIC FLEET. WE ARE ACCOMPANIED BY THREE DESTROYERS, THREE CRUISERS, AND NUMEROUS SUPPORT VESSELS. I DEMAND THAT YOU CHANGE YOUR COURSE FIFTEEN DEGREES NORTH, THAT IS ONE FIVE DEGREES NORTH, OR COUNTERMEASURES WILL BE UNDERTAKEN TO ENSURE THE SAFETY OF THIS SHIP.

CANADIANS: This is a lighthouse. Your call.

The owner and skipper of *Never Again V,* an awl-gripped flag-blue Hinckley Bermuda 40, gleaming with varnished mahogany, all sails flying and pushed by a hearty nor'wester through Merchant Row, believes he owns the goddamned world. He flew in from New York last night and he's here to have some serious fun. That idiot hauling pots ahead better scoot, chop-chop, here I come, make way! The captain of the *Susan B. Anthony,* who has felt obliged to concede right-of-way to an oil tanker or the *Cat,* thinks that blow boater might cut him some slack. This is where he works, after all, and an hour ago he had to dodge around for a parade of sea kayakers— *ten* of them lined up like a string of ducklings by a sea-adventure operator out of Bar Harbor. He's had a hard morning slamming into a right chop kicked up near Leach Rock, and his sternman—between torturing his back on the hauling wheel, pulling fifty-pound traps, and sucking diesel fumes and the stink of rotten bait— has reported a whole string of traps missing, hundreds of dollars' worth of them, their buoys no doubt cut loose by *that very asshole,* all sails drawing, bearing down on him now. That yawtsman—busy admiring the epic grandeur of granite and spray and the picturesque little lobster boats—no doubt tangled the buoys' warp around his centerboard or rudder or propeller. This intruder would be the fellow yawt club member of the sailor who languished at the fuel dock yesterday afternoon when the *Susan B. Anthony* was waiting to fill up for today's work after a hard morning on the water. Even worse than kayakers are Massachusetts hippies who tie up to the public float and walk around Stonington in rubber suits and maybe buy a granola bar. What good are those people? Not to mention that this lobsterman has a cousin who caught a guy in a big sailboat hauling one of his traps to score a free dinner under the stars with his wife and kids in the cockpit. Story was, mebbe so, mebbe not, that after that encounter a few blow boats sailing into Carver's Harbor got moose-rifle bullet holes in their Hood Easi-Stow mainsails. Story also was that a blow boat the very same color as the boat of that asshole who is still *not* changing course had attached to the propeller shaft a lobsterman-loathed device named SPURS, a weed, net, and line cutter with razor-sharp blades rotating at about three thousand rpm. With SPURS in place, the yawtsman had no need to dodge trap buoys here in Merchant Row, the most densely lobster-tapped minefield in the Gulf of Maine. That fella yonder could just run his engine in gear and cut through a dozen buoy warps during an afternoon outing, leaving a few hundred dollars worth of traps lost on the bottom.

Now someone had to give way, and the *Susan B. Anthony* gave way to *Never Again V,* whose helmsman gave a manly wave of acknowledgment as he boiled past, and received a return salute, middle finger raised and pumping up and down. This was an old story, but every now and then its reciprocating plot components build sufficient pressure for a new story, such as unfolded before my family and me a few years ago in these very waters. We were aboard *Skyfair,* a thirty-five-foot Duffy & Duffy powerboat with the lines and handling characteristics of a lobster boat. We had chartered her for two weeks out of Bucks Harbor on Eggemoggin Reach, not far from where she'd been built. We were a week into our cruise and every day seemed better than the day before. We'd been ranging the coast between Cape Rosier and Schoodic, and on this day we had spent the previous night at anchor in Burnt Coat Harbor, on Swan's Island, and we were entering Merchant Row from Toothacher Bay. We were in what is arguably the most thrilling body of water in the Gulf of Maine, which is to say in the world. Throttled back to a modest ten knots, we were making what would have seemed from the air like a drunkard's erratic path through the obstacle course of lobster pot buoys. It was a bright, bright afternoon, the light coming brilliantly off the chop, and it was so good that we were laughing at nothing. I was aboard with Priscilla and Justin and Megan, Justin's fiancée; we had bought from a fisherman a few hours earlier a piece of tuna that we meant to grill in the cock-pit. All that remained to complete our happiness was a snug anchorage, and we had many to choose among. There are dozens of islands in this archipelago—Grog and Enchanted and Hells Half Acre and Devil and Wreck—and the pink and rose and orange granite shores are ornamented by dark evergreens. This is quar-ry country, the source of the granite that built the Library of Congress, the U.S. Treasury building, the Naval Academy, the Brooklyn Bridge, and the grave of President Kennedy.

We chose McGlathery, owned by Friends of Nature and inhabited by woolly wild sheep. It was a Sunday night, and after we got settled several other boats came in, all cruising sailboats, one of them a windjammer. McGlathery has a lot of room, and everyone was respect-ing one another's territory, and talk and laughter were subdued. A couple of sea kayakers had drawn their boats up on the beach. I don't want to suggest that being at anchor in that place was like visiting a cathedral, but you see the picture. In the cockpit of *Skyfair* we had a couple of rum drinks, and about an hour before sunset we marinated the tuna and fired up the grill. We saw smoke curling in the light breeze from the transoms of a few other boats; the sea was flat calm, as it often is at that time of evening, so we had been careless about stowing our cruising paraphernalia: cameras, binoculars, plates and bowls, the rum bottle and ice bucket.

Many lobster boats have business in these waters, so hearing an engine whine nearby wasn't odd. This engine, though, was unmuffled, and it reminded me that the week before there had been lobster-boat races out of nearby Stonington. These are taken seriously by boatbuilders and lobstermen, who devote great ingenuity and much money to setting speed records. Speed in a lobster boat is not a frivolity when you are racing competitors to market, and even sailors from away have respect for the enterprise. Now it seemed we were to see a fast one up close, because it was approaching at thirty-five, maybe forty knots. We expected it to throttle back to an idle, right now! It didn't throttle back; the boat, red-hulled with gray trim, its name covered with a piece of canvas, came through the anchorage at top speed, the helmsman and sternman neither laughing nor frowning. They looked straight ahead, as though we weren't there, and did a circle around us all and headed back where they came from.

Nobody capsized in the surflike wake, but Priscilla was in the galley and a heavy pot of boiling spuds fell to the cabin sole and gave her an awful scare. We lost the tuna off the grill, and cameras fell from the cockpit table, and glasses broke, and dishes. And of course shouts of fury rose from the anchorage, and as the sun fell over McGlathery it occurred to us that we might not be welcome in these waters.

This shouldn't have come as a shock. I'm privileged to be an acquaintance of Proctor Wells, a town selectman in Phippsburg and the father, brother, son, grandson, and great-grandson of men and women who have fished out of the sea just about every kind of thing the sea provides. My elder son Nicholas has shipped out with Proctor during the past several summers, as a research scientist investigating lobsters in their larval and pre-juvenile stages, east from Boothbay to the Canadian border. Proctor's *Tenacious,* a Westec 49 rigged for ground fish, tuna, shrimp, and lobster, for an investment of half a million dollars, is as well-equipped as a working vessel gets, and Proctor puts it to the service of scientific inquiry because he has no beef with science. His curiosity about how many fish there are—and where they go, and how much fishing they can sustain—trumps his sense of partisanship. He is a man of very strong feelings—listen with him to a Yankees v. Red Sox game on a radio tuned in from Roque Island—but he takes the long view. He worries about plenty of things: Are lobster hauls sustainable? Can cod make a comeback? Do federal courts understand or care that their rulings, sometimes capricious, put families out of work? He worries a lot—as a selectman—about waterfront. The Wells family has held since colonial times a priceless piece of property in Sebasco, near the mouth of the New Meadows River. Proctor's mother lives in the big house, keeping watch over a large, working boathouse and a dock where she keeps (and uses) her tuna boat, and where Proctor and his brothers keep their boats. The value of such property to a rusticator must be dizzying to contemplate, but tax assessors sure know how to compute it. These taxes have ruined many a fisherman. Among the ones who sold out their shorefront land because they couldn't afford to keep it, some continue to fish. They live inland, in a comfortable ranch house or maybe a double-wide. To reach their lobster boats they must drive to their dinghies, pulled ashore on some generous soul's rocky beach. Scrabbling over these seaweedy rocks they earn a name—"kelp rats"—that I suspect they don't find amusing.

All of them can tell stories about those from away who have bought once-working waterfront land. Proctor tells of the lady from Chicago who bought harborfront property in Phippsburg, and after her contractor had torn down the house that came with the property and built a grander one, she moved in. The afternoon following her first morning on the water, she phoned her selectman to complain:

"Is it really necessary for those fishing boats to make so much noise when they pass our house?"

"I'm afraid it is," Proctor said.

"Well, do they have to leave so early in the morning?"

This was not the same lady who, having come to photograph the local lobster fleet, hanging off their moorings and facing southwest on a flooding tide, remarked to Proctor:

"This harbor is so tidy! Such pride the boaters show, lining up their vessels so they all point in the same direction."

Proctor laughs about these events. And when blow boaters get in trouble in his waters, well, he figures, he's been in trouble too. He tells of hauling a yar ketch aground on a ledge, dismasted, with its rudder busted, through the breakers to safety, but not before the sailboat's skipper, hooking up the towline, said he'd like to save his anchor, hooked on the leeward side of the rocks. It was a valuable anchor, evidently, had been in the family for dogs' years.

"Cut it loose when I give her the gun," Proctor responded. "Either you're coming or your stern is."

Following our unhappy dinner hour at McGlathery, late the next morning, in dense fog, we motored to Stonington with half a mind to find the harbormaster there and tell him the evil that had been done to us. We picked up a mooring at Billings Marine and saw at once a Hinckley sailboat, the *Salty Mistress,* hanging from a mooring and rafted alongside a Coast Guard cutter. The Hinckley was in bad shape, with a jagged hole amidships. An investigation seemed to be under way, so we thought to leave our complaints to another occasion and get ashore in our dinghy, buy some ice and groceries and a newspaper, and maybe eat lunch. Stonington is a busy waterfront, with many wharves and piers and docks, one of them owned by the town. We headed for it in our little ten-foot fiberglass bathtub, laden with the four of us, none petite-sized. Soon we were buzzed and nearly swamped by some teenagers in an outboard skiff, within easy view of the Coast Guard. Approaching shore we saw signs on the piers, variations of KEEP AWAY and NO DINGHY TIEUP!*

Stonington has long had a reputation as a kind of Wild East frontier town. There's still an active granite quarry on Crotch Island, mere yards across Deer Island Thorofare from the town. When quarrying was in its heyday years ago, paydays for the workers—many of them Italian—were rowdy days indeed. Collisions between fishermen and rock-cutters were epic, buckets of blood serving as impromptu boxing rings and more than a few whores as spectators.

A couple of days later we read in the Bangor newspaper that near Stonington three lobstermen had been

* A more welcoming warning on a public dinghy float nearby on Penobscot Bay reads BIRTHING LIMITED TO ONE HOUR.

injured, one of them seriously, when their thirty-five-foot powerboat plowed its bow mid-ship into a fifty-one-foot Hinckley. The owner and helmsman of the lobster boat had been injured, treated, and released from Blue Hill Hospital; his son, as the newspaper reported, "received severe facial injuries that will require plastic surgery." During the following few days, many people we encountered on Maine's waterfront had the inside scoop on what had happened in the fog three miles from Stonington. Both vessels had working radar, so they could be presumed to have seen each other before they hit. Depending on the viewpoint of the teller, lobsterman or yachtsman, we heard a story of blithe incompetence or of stubbornness exacerbated by rage. The captain of the lobster boat was said to have a violent temper, and because it was agreed that the collision occurred at higher speed than the conditions licensed, it was said by some that he had rammed and stove in the sailboat. Another version held that the sailboat captain, "from away," didn't know how to use his radar or steer his boat, and wandered into the path of the working lobster boat.

A few years later, while rooting around in some old *Bangor Daily News* clips from the winter of 2000, I came across another story about the captain of that lobster boat. A year earlier, in January and with high seas running, two miles south of Stonington, that captain had been among a posse who rescued a clammer stranded in freezing weather on a nearby island. The weather was so awful that the rescuers, pelted by freezing spray, couldn't look straight ahead to search for the unlucky clammer. Yet they kept at it till they found him. He was grateful: "It helps to have locals willing to go out there."

And the following account showed up in a Connecticut yacht club's winter newsletter, relating the outcome of the correspondent's summer cruise around waters adjacent to Stonington. He had put his sailboat hard aground on a ledge, and the lobster-boat *Nigh Duck* happened upon him and pulled him off. In the confusion of this success, *Nigh Duck* took off to resume fishing before the cruiser "could properly thank him for his good deed." Having returned to Connecticut, the rescued fellow sent a letter of thanks, together with a check made out to cash to "The Captain of the *Nigh Duck*," care of the postmaster of Stonington. A letter came back from that captain, Bill Baker: "If it makes you feel better, I pulled three boats off that ledge and a fourth not far from where you grounded. I enjoy 'rescuing' people. I didn't expect to get paid, but it will come in handy this winter."

There's no moral to be drawn here. I've got advice, though: If you're sailing through Merchant Row in the neighborhood of Stonington, keep a weather eye open for ledges and angry faces.

CRUISING: SEGUIN

We sat long at table that day, and when we went on deck about three o'clock it was raining. And the wind was beginning to blow pretty hard. We made sail at once in the direction of Boothbay, but in the course of a couple of hours the wind rose to a gale. The sea grew very rough, and almost every minute a wave would break over our vessel and, sweeping along the deck, deluge the cockpit with water.... The air was so thick with mist that we could see nothing but the raging waves around us, and could not tell where we were going, though the sloop was plunging along at a fearful rate, her bows almost continually under water and her mast opening wide cracks at every tug of the sails. There was considerable danger of the mast's going overboard. In that case we should

have been completely at the mercy of the waves, on a coast every inch of which was rock-bound, so that, if our vessel struck, she would be pounded to pieces in ten minutes.

We drove madly along, the grim old Pilot at the helm, and the anxious Skipper, arrayed in oil-skin to shed the wet, clinging to the mast and keeping a sharp lookout ahead. Suddenly the mist rose and rolled away before a sweeping blast, and then we saw Seguin lighthouse, and knew where we were. It was a superb and terrible sight—these wild reefs with the waves foaming and flashing over them, directly in our course. It was growing late, and the gale was on the increase. The sea was white with foam on the surface, but the great waves, as they came leaping and roaring at us, had a black and angry look not pleasant to behold.

—ROBERT CARTER, describing a day cruising the Maine coast, 1858

Gulls nest on the cliffs on the west side and on the northern ridge {of Seguin Island}. From this grassy knoll the poet, the painter, and the philosopher can perhaps take a sane and objective view of what otherwise seems a mad planet.

—*The Cruising Guide to the New England Coast*

Context is everything. Sixteen years after our family misadventure and rescue in the waters surrounding Ragged Island, I had an opportunity to think long and hard about another famous Maine island, Seguin, a corruption of the aboriginal word *sutquin,* meaning "place where the sea vomits." At the mouth of the Sheepscot and Kennebec Rivers, seven miles southwest of the entrance to Boothbay Harbor, Seguin Island has America's second oldest lighthouse, commissioned in 1795.

My son Justin and I were approaching Seguin five years ago. This was our first landfall following an overnight passage from Provincetown, again aboard *Blackwing* and again wrapped in fog. This time we were sailing with Loran, radar, and two GPS units; we had rendezvoused with sea buoys along the way—hitting them right on the nose—and at dawn (such as it was) we were giddy with self-satisfaction. Cocksure that we knew where we were— because we *were* there when we thought we were *there,* at Mile Ledge red bell at forty-three degrees, forty-one and five-tenths minutes north by sixty-nine degrees, forty-five and three-tenths minutes west, less than a mile south of Seguin—we paid no more attention to our electronics, relying on our utterly reliable compass. A few minutes later we heard the moan of Seguin's foghorn and imagined that we could make out, above the rocky shore just over there to port, the stone foundation of the light. We set a course for Boothbay Harbor, following in the wake of the wet and frightened Robert Carter who had sailed these waters back in 1858. Something wasn't right. The tide was flooding into the rivers, but we reckoned ourselves to be well to the east of Seguin Ledge. We weren't. First we heard surf breaking and then we saw the ledge dead ahead. Just in time I cranked the wheel and fell off the wind to deep water. After I gave the helm to Justin, I studied NOAA chart 13293. I had to squint to read it, but written in purple on the chart, right between Seguin Island and Seguin Ledge, and just at an outcropping called Ellingwood Rock, was the declaration LOCAL MAGNETIC DISTURBANCE (SEE NOTE). I found the note: "Differences of as much as eight degrees from the normal variation have been observed in an area around Ellingwood Rock for approximately one nautical mile in all directions." You might ask, what's eight degrees between sailors and ledges? A lot. Enough to haul you up on Tom Rock or The Sisters or Black Rocks or White Ledge or Jackknife Ledge. Relying on a compass in this case is about as reliable as a hunch. I consulted my electronics again, and left them blinking and buzzing warnings at us until we were moored at Boothbay Harbor.

In the interest of commercial shipping crossing the Atlantic and sailing the coast to and from Portland, a light was called for to mitigate the Seguin neighborhood's shipwrecking perils. Local merchants petitioned for this light, and it was ordered by President George Washington at a cost of $6,300. It was even more impressive then than now, rising 186 feet, the highest light in Maine. The first keeper, a Frenchman who served against the lobster-backs in the Revolution, was paid two hundred dollars a year—a good deal more than Abbie Burgess's dad got much later for keeping Matinicus Light, but a good deal less than Seguin's keeper felt he deserved. He had a point. In his first year at the light storms broke up his two boats and a canoe; the larger of his boats was valued at three hundred dollars. A short time later, history records, John Polereczky died "penniless and boatless" on Seguin. The damp, mildewed, and maundering wooden structure—beset by fog and storm-driven spray—began to rot and collapse as soon as it was erected. In 1842 it was replaced by a stone structure, now painted white with a black lens-house and attached dwelling. In 1857 Seguin light received Maine's only First Order Fresnel lens, the most powerful light on the coast. Fresnel's lenses, designed in 1822 by Augustin Fresnel and manufactured in Paris, are optical masterpieces of ingenuity, graded in order of their size, cost, and complexity from First Order (called "hyper radiants") to Sixth. Seguin's lens, weighing three tons and standing twice the height of a keeper, valued at eight million dollars, was saved by the intervention of a local lobsterman from being dismantled by the Coast Guard in the 1980s. Tended and financially supported privately by Friends of Seguin Island in Bath, one of the many salvation and restoration projects along this coast, the light is lit by a couple of thousand-watt bulbs—only ten times the power of a household bulb—and focuses its rays to an intensity of four million candle-power, casting its beam eighteen miles. (In earlier days it managed a similar range using lamps lit by sperm oil, lard, and kerosene.) It does this by a dauntingly complex arrangement of more than a thousand crystal prisms and bull's-eye lenses mounted in a brass frame. In the infancy of Maine's lighthouses they all cast a single white beam, creating a dazzling and bewildering string of light along the coast. To distinguish between these lights, colored lenses were tried, radically reducing their range. The solution was the creation of flash patterns, a periodicity peculiar to each light and published in the Coast Guard's *Light List* under the rubric "light characteristics." Each light has its flash-and-eclipse interval, a repetition pattern controlled by a clockwork mechanism—driving huge counterweights and needing to be wound several times per day—comprising shutters mounted on low-friction rails circling the Fresnel lens. Seguin's characteristic used to be one second lit followed by one second eclipsed. Today, owing to its blue-ribbon place of honor in the lighthouse pantheon, it beams white and steady; its fog signal sounds two brays every twenty seconds.

With as much as 2,374 hours of fogginess (27 percent of a year's total hours), Seguin needed a potent fog signal. The original bell couldn't be heard above pounding surf, so it was replaced by a steam-driven whistle, which was replaced by a diaphone horn so powerful that its concussive blast, heard fourteen miles distant in Bath, extinguished kerosene lamps and knocked seagulls out of the air.

The more prominent the light, the grislier the ghost story. Seguin's could have inspired fellow Mainer Stephen King to dream up *The Shining*. It seems that during the nineteenth century the keeper's wife had a piano on the island, and on that piano she played a single song over and over. (All work and no play makes Jack a dull boy?) The keeper destroyed the piano with an ax, then killed the pianist, and then himself. Some say that the tune drifts to the mainland on quiet nights.

The music I remember is in a deeper octave, the grave lowing of the Seguin horn through the fog. And welcomed in my memory I can see on a clear night from the entrance to Boothbay Harbor six lights, a necklace of steadfastness, flashing in code their warnings and welcomes, announcing unambiguously the mariner's situation.

THE GALLANT KENNEBEC

Monday being the 17th of August Capt. Popham in his shallop with thirty others and Capt. Gilbert in his ship's boat accompanied with eighteen other persons departed early in the morning from their ships and sailed up the River of Sagadahoc for to view the river and also to see where they might find the most convenient place for their plantation myself being with Capt. Gilbert. So we sailed up into this river near fourteen leagues and found it to be a most gallant river very broad and of a good depth …{with an} abundance of great fish in it leaping above the water on each side of us as we sailed. *

— ATTRIBUTED TO JAMES DAVIES, NAVIGATOR OF RALEIGH
GILBERT'S *Mary and John,* 1607

* I have modernized perplexing spelling, but left diction and syntax as composed.

At the mouth of Maine's most storied river, Popham Beach curves three miles southwest. Winter gales reshape its crescent contour, piling and gnawing the surf-slammed dunes at the high tide line, and summer breezes comb the dune grass into cowlicks garlanded with beach rose, but despite the sand's mutability, the grandeur of this shoreline's scale is fundamental. You'd have to travel to the Bay of Fundy or to the south coast of Brittany to approximate so theatrical a tidal effect. As I write this in 2004 the high tide line at Popham Beach is mere feet from the dunes, which took a grievous beating last winter, but at low tide the fine sand shimmers almost to the horizon and one can walk a quarter-mile to Fox or Wood Islands. Popham is often foggy, even when the sun shines half a mile inland, and when mist obscures the islands offshore—Pond Island lighting the entrance of the Kennebec and nearby Seguin horning its "keep away!"—it's almost possible to imagine what it was like in 1607 to close in on this turbulent, bristling coast aboard the *Gift of God,* threading through breaking surf without detailed charts or navigational aids except for a compass. The tidal set hereabouts—a consequence of water ebbing every six hours from the Kennebec at as much as six knots—could drive a stranger on any number of nearby ledges, not least of them Seguin Ledge, rather than helping entrance to the mouth of the river known by Indians and settlers as Sagadahoc.

The *Gift of God,* commanded by George Popham, was accompanied by the *Mary and John,* under Raleigh Gilbert, nephew of Sir Walter Raleigh. The 120 settlers—noblemen and vagrants, all men and boys—had sailed from England on May 31 with the blessing of James I, who had authorized the establishment of two Virginia colonies: the southern in Jamestown.* After a layover in the Azores, the settlers of the northern Virginia outpost arrived at Sabino Head at the mouth of the river on August 19. They named their colony Fort St. George and raised over it the emblem of England's dragon-slaying patron saint, a flag bearing the red cross on a white field. The newcomers immediately found plenty to eat. Fish, of course, crowded the mouth of the river: striped bass, bluefish, flounder, fat salmon, haddock, sturgeon, lobsters, and huge cod. Oysters were so abundant that mounds of shells, the detritus of hundreds of years worth of Native American feasts along the banks of the nearby Damariscotta River, tower twenty-five feet high. These cliffs each contain an estimated forty-five million cubic feet of

* The "comeoverers," as they're sometimes named, were a mixed lot. A principal sponsor of Popham's venture was his brother, Sir John, a member of Parliament and Lord Chief Justice, an avid advocate of deportation to rid Britain of rogues and vagabonds. Among these were those skilled enough as artisans and craftsmen to build a nice little ship.

oyster shells. Along the Kennebec, Popham and his crew routinely found oysters almost a foot long. The soil too was rich, and onions and grapes, walnuts and hops, peas and barley flourished. These newcomers were no dreamers yearning to build a city upon a hill but venture capitalists. The leery colonizers' first project on going ashore was to engineer their escape, building a pinnace—a small schooner which they named the *Virginia of Sagadahoc*. Pangloss would celebrate this urgent shipbuilding enterprise as the fruit of curiosity: The fifty-footer was shoal enough to carry explorers into bays and up rivers. A realist would understand that the *Virginia* was built to carry the newcomers the hell away from fog, tidal rips, and "the sea vomits" should elsewhere beckon.

Jumping forward to the "Great Migration" (1630–40), the situation of a settler aboard the *Angel Gabriel* illuminates the Pophamites's dilemma. This fellow was one John Bayeley, and a historian researching the colonial history of the Bayeley family could not at first fathom why this weaver had abandoned his beloved wife, son, and daughters in England for the remaining sixteen years of his life after arriving off Pemaquid Point, on August 14, 1635, following a passage of forty-two days from Milford Haven, Wales. The *Angel Gabriel* was a square-rigged bark of 240 tons, armed with more than a dozen cannon and a hundred or so passengers who, according to the journal of their contemporary Richard Mather, were mostly "loving and godly Christians." They had had a rough and eventful crossing, encountering a Turkish pirate. They killed and boated a porpoise for "marvelous merry sport" at the end of June, the day after the Sabbath, and for this "delightful recreation [of] taking and opening ye huge and strange fish" the shipmates thanked their Maker. Soon smallpox infected those aboard the *Angel Gabriel,* and rough seas tossed them and storms lashed them and seasickness discouraged them.* But they found their ledge-strewn landfall and dropped anchor. Shortly after midnight of that August 15 the wind veered from the southwest to northeast and up blew a hurricane. Settlers along the coast recorded that crops were mowed down, the tide surged to twenty feet above the normal high in Boston. Indians climbed trees to save themselves from drowning, and many of these

* Richard Mather was the father of Increase and grandfather of Cotton. "But lest we should grow secure and neglect ye Lord through abundance of prosperity, our wise and loving God was pleased on Monday morning [August 3rd] ... to exercise us with a sore storm and tempest of wind ... and our seamen were forced to let down all ye sails, and ye ship was so tossed with fearful mountains and valleys of water, as if we should have been overwhelmed & swallowed up. But ye lasted not long, for at our poor prayers, ye Lord was pleased to magnify his mercy in assuaging ye wind & seas again about sun rising...." As the Book warns, what He giveth on Monday He also taketh away a week from Saturday.

great trees were snapped like toothpicks. Increase Mather's *Remarkable Providences,* making later use of his father Richard's journal, tells that the furious storm "threw down (either breaking them off by the bole or plucking them up by the roots) thousands of great trees." William Bradford, of Plymouth, rated it "such a mighty storm of wind and rain as none living in these parts, either English or Indian, ever saw." The *Angel Gabriel* was hurled on the rocks of Pemaquid and smashed to toothpicks. Only five, at most seven, among the company died; the rest were carried by caprice ashore but all lost their livestock and provisions and family heirlooms. At great cost each comeoverer had brought a year's supplies. In addition to cattle, these included farming tools, flour, gunpowder, musket shot, household furnishings, and even upper body armor (in case the French got up to mischief). John Bayeley refused ever to board a boat again. His report of his experience, carried to his wife in England, was so persuasively discouraging that she followed his example. He brings to mind the legendary ambition, as old as Homer's *Odyssey,* provoked in weather-beaten seafarers who have experienced enough water, to row ashore, shoulder an oar, and walk inland until someone, spying the oar, asks "What's that thing?" Jolly legends, in the form of sea chanteys or fo'c's'le gams, promise that the oar-ignorant place is a sweet paradise,

Fiddlers' Green, where fish jump into your frying pan, the skipper brews tea for his crew, the girls are all pretty, the beer is on the house, and bottles of rum lie around on the ground, ripe as pumpkins for the plucking.

Back at Popham Colony, years before the *Angel Gabriel* was lost, the inhabitants knew all too well what an oar was. They had reached their landfall in search of gold, silver, and—as always—a northwest passage to China and the Indies. As the summer gave way to autumn, and leaves fell from the hardwoods, and frost nipped shrewdly inside the settlers' straw and mud huts, the newcomers dreamed of heading south to Virginia or back to England. Those first colonizers might be regarded as Mainers think of summer folk "from away," fair-weather friends lately titled "rusticators." Historians divide as to whether the winter of 1607–08 was insufferable or merely ghastly. The late Robert P. Tristram Coffin, a Pulitzer Prize–winning poet and himself a descendant of early Maine settlers, was unimpressed by the meteorological record: "The winter was one of the robust kind, such as only Maine can grow. These first Kennebec men took in their belts and scrabbled for food. It was hard sledding." Bill Caldwell's estimation in *Rivers of Fortune* is more dire. The 120 settlers had raised their flimsy shelters in the face of the winter's winds and the winter "was especially cold." He is supported in his judgment by John Davies, who had the advantage of experiencing that winter and the disadvantage of having no other Maine winters to which to contrast it. Davies, comparing Popham with the "extraordinary frost felt in most parts of Europe," describes the Maine winter as "extremely unseasonable" and "vehement, by which no boat could stir on any business." It was surely colder than they had expected: Fort St. George lay along the latitude (forty-three degrees north) of the south of France, but Cannes it was not. Louis B. Wright, in his *Atlantic Frontier,* tells that the English insisted on believing that the climate of Maine was "salubrious and that all the fruits and spices of England would grow there." Louise Rich quotes from a Popham colonist's diary of January 18, 1608: "There was in the space of seven hours 'thunder, lightning, rain, frost, snow in all abundance, the last continuing.' They assumed that this was typical, and they were right."

The poor newcomers couldn't even entice their firewood to burn: It was as green as their horns. For whatever additional reasons—failure to find gold or silver, the ravages of scurvy, fear of the natives or the belligerent French, ice floes piling up on the river, the unwelcome sight of snow crusting the beach that seemed so pretty in August—more than half the settlers sailed away "in disgust and disappointment" aboard the *Virginia of*

Sagadahoc as soon as the spring thaw set them free. George Popham, brother of England's Lord Chief Justice, "unwieldy with fat," "timorously fearful to offend," and almost eighty when he arrived at Fort St. George, had died during the Maine winter, and news came from England that the second-in-command, Raleigh Gilbert, had inherited a fortune, which he was impatient to commence enjoying.* Back in England the escapees told such scarifying tales of winter hardship and native savagery that "all former hopes were frozen to death," in the words of Gorges. In the bitter aftermath of the fiasco came blame and lawsuits and what economic historians of market manias and cutthroat speculation term "revulsion."

---

* Sir Ferdinando Gorges was the flamboyant chief among the self-styled "Gentlemen Adventurers" who prompted and invested in the principal explorations of the Maine coast during the early seventeenth century. He had been taken prisoner during the Battle of the Spanish Armada at the age of twenty-one; a year later he distinguished himself with his sword-handling during the siege of Rouen and was knighted there at twenty-three. Having largely financed Fort St. George, he had a dyspeptic opinion of his business colleague: Raleigh Gilbert, Gorges wrote, lived loosely, was "desirous of supremacy in rule, prompt to sensuality, with little zeal in religion, humorous, headstrong, and of small judgement." Gilbert was in his mid-twenties in 1607, and believed by at least one historian to have high-hatted the elder and bureaucratically superior George Popham. Archaeological explorations of the Popham Colony site have revealed the rubble of Gilbert's expensive taste: shards of liquor bottles, pieces of a Venetian wine glass, and buttons from a luxurious waistcoat. For his part, the censorious Sir Ferdinando's fingers remained in many an American pie: In 1635 he had boarded the *Angel Gabriel* at Bristol to bid farewell to crew and passengers. He was not a good-luck charm.

Colonists gave a pass to New England till a dozen years later, when the *Mayflower* carried Pilgrims to Plymouth. The fifty-five left behind in 1608 are lost to history. Coffin doesn't much fret about them: "They were tough customers and could have made their beds anywhere." Their contemporary John Aubrey declared that the colony was a gang of vagabonds "stocked out of all the gaols of England." Gorges was disgusted with the crew he sent out to make his name and fortune. They split into squabbling factions, each slandering the other, "even to the Savages." Indeed, in Gorges' distempered view, the English were "worse than the very Savages, impudently and openly lying with their Women" (that would be the Indians' women) and "teaching their Men to drinke drunke, to swear and blaspheme in the name of God." The Abnaki, in their turn, were bored unto numbness by frequent Church of England sermons, which they were forced to endure in return for lunch or dinner at the fort.* The colonizers liked to march around

* James Davies witnessed this occasion: "There came two canoes to the fort, in which were Nahanada and his wife, and Skidwares [familiar with English church custom: see account below of his kidnap and removal to London], and the Basshabes brother, and one other called Amenquin, a sagamore; all whom the president [George Popham] feasted and entertained with all kindness, both that day and the next, which being Sunday, the president carried them with him to the place of public prayers, which they were at both morning and evening, attending with great reverence and silence."

on a hot late summer day in armor, to intimidate their put-upon neighbors. These miscreants were disinclined to honor the niceties of fair play in their trade with the Abnaki (two shillings in beads were traded for beaver pelts to be sold in London, to make hats much in fashion, for one hundred pounds sterling). When the colonists were not in the bartering vein, they shut the gates of their fort and sent dogs to threaten the Abnaki who had come to trade. These Indians, believed by the pinchfist settlers to be "exceedingly subtle and cunning," knew themselves as the Dawn People and valued generosity as their chief social virtue. Justly stung by sellers' remorse, they evidently raided the settlers' food supplies and burned down the stockade.* Three years later the ruins of Fort St. George were visited by a Jesuit

---

* Three years earlier, during an exploration of Muscongus Bay, just east of Pemaquid, George Waymouth and his crew aboard *Archangel* had cunningly abused the natives' hospitality; after trading trinkets for otter, beaver, and marten skins, they hoodwinked them with a spurious display of magic, using a magnetic rock—used to remagnetize the *Archangel*'s compass—to cause a knife to spin and a magnetized sword blade to lift a stitching needle. This they did to awe the Abnaki, so that they might "love and fear us," as James Rosier confessed to his diary. On the pretext of delivering some celebrated English cooking as a gift, Waymouth's crew rendezvoused with a small party of Indians on the beach at Allen Island, where they grabbed by their long hair (the Abnaki warriors were naked) and kidnapped five "savages," to be carried to England to edify and amuse society. From the point of view of Rosier, these exotic fellows "never seemed discontented with us, but very tractable, loving and willing." They learned English, enabling them to explain to their credulous hosts

priest, Father Pierre Biard, who recorded the Abnaki's ill-use by the settlers, whom they claimed to have driven away owing to the "outrages they had experienced from these English." (For their part, the Jesuits used as a platform for their program of conversion an inventory of the Lord Jesus Christ's grievances against the English. The Abnaki were taught that Jesus was French, as was of course the Virgin. The English crucified Him and those who would serve Him would condemn and attack the English.) The customs of the Abnaki were vividly captured a few decades later by John Josselyn, an English naturalist and systematic visitor to this part of the coast. He described the natives as tall, with good posture and very white teeth, clean-shaven and keen of sight. He reports their purposeful transience, "always removing from one place to another for conveniency of food ... I have seen half a hundred of their Wigwams together in a piece of ground and ... within a day or two, or a week, they have been all dispersed." He described the Abnaki diet— including bear meat and venison and eggs and roasted lobsters and dried moose-tongues, "which they esteem a dish for a Sagamor." The Abnaki "have prodigious stomachs,

how Abnaki made cream and butter by milking deer and reindeer, evidently keeping straight faces during the lecture. A principal Abnaki spirit, feared and revered for his shrewdness, was named Gluskap. The name, as Neil Rolde notes, means in our language "Liar." Four of the captives were returned to Maine, owing to their utility as guides and translators.

devouring a great deal ... never giving over eating as long as they have it, between meals spending their time in sleep till the next kettleful is boiled.... If they have none of this, as sometimes it falleth out (being a very careless people not providing against the storms of want and tempest of necessity) they make use of Sir Francis Drake's remedy for hunger, go to sleep."

The Popham colonists were hungry but too cold to sleep. Yet they would leave a legacy. The *Virginia,* the first ship built on the Kennebec, was a harbinger of many more to come. By the mid-nineteenth century Maine's busiest river would send more ships to more ports around the world than any place on the planet. The reason is not difficult to divine. The Popham colonists included at least one shipwright well equipped with axes and knives, also saws and adzes, scrapers, mauls, and caulking irons used to pound tarred hemp into the seams between a ship's planks. But the vein of plenty the settlers discovered right before their eyes, and more precious than the silver mines they sought, was the river realm's astonishing vegetation; they came ashore in the midst of a shipwright's Eden, with great stands of white pine (called "hackamack" by the Indians and juniper by the newcomers), perfect for masts. For keels there was oak; for ribs and stems and decks there was a bounty of cedar, spruce, maple, and elm.

A contemporary community of enthusiastic historians and boat-builders and naval architects has undertaken to build a replica, scheduled to be launched in 2007. Their *Virginia,* being constructed in Phippsburg, the present-day town where the Popham Colony was located, is a covered-deck barkentine of fifty feet, with a beam of fourteen feet six inches. It is known that the sturdy ship made passages up and down the colonial coast trading in furs and fish, and ran tobacco from Virginia to England, before being wrecked off the coast of Ireland (according to Louise Rich) or ending her days "with good English-men chained in it, among the Barbary pirates" (according to Coffin). Much educated guesswork, the outcome of research and goodly hunch, is going into the *Virginia's* specifications, but what is known in detail about the ships and boats and yachts that followed down the Kennebec is solid, and impressive.

That the Popham Colony seemed to its sponsors to be such an unalloyed failure may have been coastal Maine's ultimate good luck. England resigned itself to the paucity near the Kennebec of precious metals to be mined. So mid-coast Maine was left to the fishermen who had used its waters long before Popham and Gilbert planted their king's flag at Fort St. George. In fact, European fishermen were so well established in the Gulf of Maine that the Abnaki were found by France's early explorers to know a kind of pidgin Basque, which they'd learned from Spaniards come from the Bay of Biscay to catch and salt cod.* Monhegan was a fishing camp long before the Popham Colony was attempted. And Damariscove Island, near the mouths of the Sheepscot and Kennebec Rivers, was a busy port of call for transient fishermen. After the Virginia colony took root, its seafaring merchants made their way up the coast to Damariscove to trade for fish, and eventually in other commodities. One contemporary noted that servants brought to Damariscove were "sold up and down like horses." Christopher Levett, an English visitor to the coast a few years after Popham Colony failed, was surprised to be addressed as "cozen Levett" by a sagamore of the Abnaki, and to learn that the sagamore's preferred curse was "a pox on his hounds!"

The English Parliament, responsive to the appetite of its belligerent navy for seamen, regarded its colonial fisheries as an apprenticeship for its crews, and encouraged the enterprise of catching and curing fish by declaring Wednesdays and Saturdays to be "fish days" at

---

* Some few mythologizing amateur archaeologists are derided by their sober peers for having suggested that rune stones near Popham Beach, and elsewhere in Maine, might bear the marks of a visit by Leif Eriksson's crew as early as 1114. In *The Story of Mount Desert Island,* Samuel Eliot Morison notes that the credulous continue to hunt for Norse treasure with Geiger counters, "which will give them plenty of exercise and do no harm."

home. Cod was the staple: Easy to cure by simple drying (owing to its low fat content), Atlantic cod were so plentiful in the Gulf of Maine that the bottom feeders—gulping whole lobsters and squid at their preferred depth of twenty to more than a hundred fathoms, and growing themselves as fat as two hundred pounds and as long as six feet—were difficult not to catch. Fishermen are naturally secretive, but the plenty being harvested from the Gulf of Maine and its rivers did not go long unnoticed, inasmuch as fishermen are also naturally self-celebrating as to the size of their catch. James Rosier, in his 1605 expedition with George Waymouth, boasted of having caught in a few hours, using three hooks baited with cod, "fish enough for our whole Company for three days." By 1620 the cod catch was so spectacular that a single shipment of 173,000 fish in that year from Monhegan weighed more than 170 tons and fetched at market $75,000.

Also impossible to disregard was the Kennebec's richness of forests. The experience of having built the *Virginia,* straight-masted and sturdy, made more than a few pennies drop across the sea, and some of them dropped at the court of King James. (A London lawsuit in the messy aftermath of the failure of the Popham Colony specified that the *Gift of God* had interrupted its rescue of the colonists by a detour to the Azores to unload and sell a shipment of thirty-three masts.) Having recently survived the Spanish Armada, the British Navy was in urgent need of warships, and England's forests were running low on old-growth trees suitable for masts. England, requiring new masts as America today needs oil, was already at the mercy of imports, buying pricey timber from Scandinavia. There for the cutting was such an abundance of huge first-growth white pines—as great as thirty-eight inches in diameter and 115 feet in height—that King James marked them as his own personal best, engraving them with the sign of a broad arrow axed with three strokes into their trunks. This Broad Arrow Policy, at first applied only to trees—usually white pines exceeding two feet in diameter at a height of one foot from the ground—reserved for the crown's ships, soon inclined toward wanton claims. By the end of the seventeenth century colonial agents of the king were scratching broad arrows on the masts of American-built and American-owned ships that had unluckily caught the agents' fancy while sailing in American waters.

A singular synergy was begun. To fish and to trade fish, ships were needed. For the ships timber was needed. As the forests were cleared along the banks of the Kennebec, farming flourished. An auxiliary benefit of the furious chopping and sawing was the comforting illusion of security: The cunning savages who used the forests to ambush white men and women would be foiled by clear-cutting. (The Abnaki, depending in their attacks on surprise, inasmuch as they were invariably outgunned, were reflexively accused of treachery, a charge akin to our country's distaste for the tactics of the Vietcong.) Bath, like other towns along the river, had a "mast depot." Huge masts were loaded aboard ships bound for England through ports cut in the bow or stern of the ship. Once loaded, the vessel's port was planked over and caulked tight. The cutting of white pine, begun in earnest in the 1630s, ended in the exhaustion of the resource by the 1800s.

English traders working the Kennebec and its neighboring region played the Native Americans as best they could. They continued to angle for beaver pelts, shipping tons of them to England during the 1630s. The slick settlers were no match for London slickers, who managed to keep the New World traders so deeply in debt to the company store that "despite beaver exports worth ten thousand pounds, they still owed twelve hundred pounds to their creditors," as Neil Rolde tells, quoting William Bradford to the effect that Bradford's fellow-colonial bumpkins had been "hoodwincte."

What happened to the Abnaki was more ruinous than any hoodwinking. That history of imperial greed, violence, and cynicism is not my subject in these pages, thanks be. All by now know the litany: rum, gunpowder, smallpoxed blankets, ethnic cleansing, misappropriation in the guise of godly zeal, false dealing, broken promises. The white settlers' inventory of iniquities spurred by ungoverned appetite was played out here as elsewhere on our continent, according to the iron laws of Manifest Destiny. Now the scarce and scattered survivors of the Algonquin Nation* along Maine's coast angle for recompense in the form of gambling casinos or liquid natural gas depots Down East. But when the Kennebec was beginning its heyday of shipbuilding, and Bath was a showplace of luxurious colonial architecture, the Abnaki—with the encouragement of the French (*toujours*)—burned the town to the ground, not in a single conflagration but in serial raids. Never mind, it was thriving so grandly that Bath rebuilt itself into a showplace of Federal architecture. Across the river from Bath, in Woolwich, at Days Ferry, the Abnaki attacked the Hammond family, killed the father and son and marched Mrs. Hammond and her young children to Quebec, where they were sold as slaves to the French, who preferred to title their slaves "converts." Such raids were commonplace, as routine as terrorism in the

* The Abnaki, which means "whitening sky at daybreak," is a confederacy of tribes, including Passamaquoddy, Penobscot, Norridgewock, and Malecite.

Middle East, during the hundred years of war between the French and English, and the Kennebec, marking a boundary between the enemies, was liable to flare up at any time between 1675 and 1763. When these wars began, there were an estimated three thousand Abnaki in Maine and six thousand Maine settlers, of whom a thousand were killed and many hundreds taken captive. The settlers, increasingly aggressive in their own raids, more than evened the score during the final fifty years of the struggle, decimating the coastal Maine tribes. When the French settled with the English at the Treaty of Paris, the bloodshed ended at once. As usual, the ones in the middle had been torn apart.

DURING THE 1800S THE KENNEBEC WAS ONE OF THE most productive shipbuilding centers in the world. Bath was the young country's fifth busiest port and Kennebec vessels, accounting for one-quarter of all registered tonnage among Maine traders just before the Civil War, traversed the globe. In *Lighthouses of Maine,* Bill Caldwell quotes a couple of snippets taken from the *Bath Daily Times* of the 1880s, routine reports of comings and goings on the Kennebec: "Yesterday on the passenger steamer *Henry Morrison,* we counted 27 schooners at Bath, 13 more between Bath and

Richmond, 55 more between Richmond and Hallowell, and two more docking at Augusta." The other item reports that during March 1884, a single month, "the in-and-out traffic on the Kennebec was 892 vessels," comprising schooners (757), sloops (39), barks (7), brigs (3), and steamers (86).

Maine didn't produce an impressive variety of goods, but what it did provide was in wide demand: pine masts and timber, limestone and granite, and later, when its mills and factories were thriving, wool and shoes. New England sassafras root was prized as a specific against the French pox, the name the English of course gave to syphilis. Ships from Maine would typically journey south to Charleston or Savannah and pick up cotton, before crossing to Liverpool, say, to unload this freight and return to New England with paying passengers. Kennebec ships carried spruce and pine for railroad ties to the treeless pampas, returning from the Rio Plata with ox hides to supply Maine's shoe factories; these skins, even those that had been tanned, stunk something awful, and green hides, swarming with insects, were almost as miserable a cargo as the beef bones brought back from the pampas to be ground into fertilizer. From the west coast of South America, Maine vessels fetched guano, so it was little wonder that despite Maine's strict laws against slaving, many a captain and crew did a bit of outlaw trading. In a typical trade with the West Indies, a ship might take down salted cod and pine boards, returning with sugar, rum, molasses, cigars, and—after a detour to a southern port—human beings. From Africa they brought palm oil, gold dust, and ivory. To China the tall ships took opium and furs, returning with chinaware and tea. From India they fetched linseed, indigo, jute for gunnysacks, and cockroaches huge enough to terrify a Boston waterfront dog; to India—most remarkable cargo of all—they carried Kennebec ice. The first shipment of ice from New England to Calcutta was tried in May 1833, and after a passage of six months, twenty thousand miles aboard the *Tuscany,* two-thirds of the 180-ton cargo arrived still frozen.*

Along the Kennebec ice was big business. One can see the simple appeal once the transaction has been described, but whoever first reckoned to peddle ice to people jaded by sunshine has to have been a Yankee, with Yankee ingenuity. The pioneer of the ice trade was a Bostonian, Frederic Tudor, who cut blocks of frozen

* Local natives, having bought the novel merchandise, left it in the sun to show it off to jealous neighbors, and demanded a full refund when the inevitable occurred. Still, the English in India quickly took to ice, and to the Baldwin apples shipped from Boston buried in the refrigerated holds. Ice became the foundation of the lively New England–India trade, a trade so valued (note the ubiquity of India Street and India Wharf in local seaports) that Samuel Eliot Morison reports that "it used to be said of a pretty, well-bred girl, 'She's good enough to marry an East-India Cap'n.'"

water from his Massachusetts pond in Saugus, hauled three hundred tons of it by teams of horses to nearby Charlestown, and shipped it by his brig *Favorite* from Boston to Martinique during a yellow fever epidemic there in 1805. Amid gales of laughter from Boston's competing merchants, Tudor's first go at the enterprise put him in the hole, an almost life-changing loss. Melting was a problem, of course, and the novelty of the initiative didn't help. But Tudor, in his twenties, was startlingly indifferent to the opinions of others, and he tried again. Following the War of 1812, the English government forgave Tudor's payment of colonial port duties and granted him monopolies in the ice trade to Jamaica. The Tudor Company received a similar dispensation from Spain in return for shipping ice to Havana (Tudor wrote, "drink, Spaniards, and be cool," so that he might keep himself warm and comfy), and soon it was competing with rival New England enterprises to sell ice to the colonies of Barbados, Trinidad, and Martinique. Added to these markets, Tudor and his competitors sold ice to consumers in Baltimore, Charleston, Savannah, and New Orleans. At first all of these markets were served from ships home-ported in Boston, but by 1820 word of the alchemy that was translating a wintertime nuisance into a valued commodity had spread north and east, and Maine made its fruitful entry into the ice boom.

The creation myth has an air of apocrypha about it, but responsible historians tell it, so here goes, from William Hutchinson Rowe's *Maritime History of Maine:*

> *Sometime around 1820, William Bradstreet came up the Kennebec in his little 125-ton brig* Orion. *It was late in the fall, and she was frozen in at Dearborn's wharf in what was then Pittston. When the river broke up in the spring and the heavy cakes of ice floated about the brig, they were pulled aboard and stowed in the hold, and the* Orion *sailed for Baltimore with a cargo that cost nothing and sold for $700. This was the first shipment of "Kennebec River Ice," a name soon to be familiar the world over. It was a business which put millions of dollars into the pockets of Maine farmers, merchants, and shipowners. For years it was Maine's surest crop. In 1890, when the State House was remodeled, a picture {of an ice harvester} was placed on the stained-glass windows of the old senate chamber.*

By the 1830s icehouses were being built all along both banks of the Kennebec, below the head of navigation at Augusta and above Thorne Point in north Bath, where the sea's tidal reach ceases to salt the water. In the harvest's heyday half a century later, many of these structures would be airplane-hangar huge, as grand as seven hundred feet in length, forty feet wide, and stacked thirty feet to their eaves with frozen blocks. Farmers had earlier built small ice sheds to preserve butter, milk, meat. The huge riverside ice warehouses were often double-walled structures, with sawdust between the walls serving as insulation, assisted by straw or spruce boughs laid under and over the slabs of ice—uniformly twenty-two by forty-four inches and a foot thick—cut from the river. Kennebec ice—which competed with Penobscot River and Hudson River ice—was prized for its assumptive purity. The river enjoyed the profitable outcome of brand recognition: The product, clear and without bubbles, was known as "Kennebec diamonds." Encouraged by reliably bitter winter temperatures, an idle workforce of farmers educated in the methods of food preservation and the tools of harvesting, with teams of horses and neighboring lumberjacks and sawyers to cut ice, enjoyed their situation near a river up which deep-draft sailing ships could venture. Gently sloping riverbanks combined with deep water close to shore made for a geographic characteristic as favorable to ice loading as to shipbuilding. An abundance of sawmills along the river shaped timber to shipbuilders and sold sawdust to icehouses.

F. H. Forbes, in *Scribner's Monthly Magazine,* entertainingly narrates the history of New England's ice trade, nearing its peak as he wrote in 1875. To stimulate the already far-flung and avid market for ice to preserve butter and to cool fevers and to make iced drinks and ice cream, in 1842 Jacob Hittinger, a Boston speculator in Maine ice harvests, invaded the land of warm bitter and scotch whiskey neat. This was a meticulously planned attack, undertaken with an advance guard of American bartenders whom Hittinger had "initiated into the mysteries of mixing juleps, smashes, cocktails, and other drinks known only in Yankeeland." Preceding the arrival of the ice-laden bark *Sharon* at a Thames wharf, Hittinger used his letters of introduction to officers of the better London clubs to display his barkeeps' wiles and lure the clubmen from their tepid beverages. Despite an encouraging brush fire of publicity from Fleet Street, then as now longing for novelty, nothing was doing. Ice "appeared to them a strange fish that no one dared to touch," as Hittinger told Forbes:

> *My feelings were just about the temperature of my ice, and wasting as rapidly. At last I was introduced to the Chairman or President of the Fishmongers' Association, an association which I was not long in discovering had the merit of wealth, if not social position. He was sociable, and seemed to comprehend my*

position if I didn't his. Matters were soon arranged;
a magnificent hall or saloon had been secured; I
ascertained that my barkeepers, through constant
drill, had attained the correct sleight of hand in
mixing the drinks. The hour had arrived. The hall
was long and brilliantly lighted. After the company
was seated, the chairman introduced me and the sub-
ject of the evening's discussion. Now, thought I, I am
all right. At a given signal the well-trained waiters
appeared, laden with the different drinks. The effect
was gorgeous, and I expected an ovation that no
Yankee had ever had. But, alas!...

Hittinger, after a hasty embarkation for Boston, tallied his substantial losses. England had used ice before Hittinger's arrival, and would use it again, sparingly, but it fished its paltry cubes out of its own ponds and lakes, or imported them from Norway.

Tudor was nothing if not a promoter, and to drum up business in hot-weather ports he not only entered into ruinous price wars with his competitors but supplied the know-how and manpower to build icehouses in which to store the commodity. Other speculations in this product ended badly: Tudor borrowed three thousand dollars at 40 percent to ship an ice-packed cargo of tropical fruit from Cuba to Boston, but the dunnage of marsh hay packed too tightly in the ship's hold began to smoke, threatening spontaneous combustion, and was jettisoned. On his return to Boston, Tudor wrote, his "creditors at once became active."

The ice market was elsewhere. New York consumed as much as a million tons per year. By the 1880s ice was only incidentally a luxury in the big cities. It preserved food and medicine from spoiling, rescuing sweltering tenement dwellers as well as nabobs from epidemics, and was considered late in the nineteenth century by the urban poor to be a staple as necessary as bread and milk. In 1886 the Kennebec shipped south a million tons, carried on a thousand ships, sold at ten dollars per ton, picked up aboard the vessel. When the mild winter south of Maine prevented the Hudson from freezing in 1872, there was jubilation from Bath to Augusta.*

Robert P. Tristram Coffin, born in 1892 on a saltwater farm southeast of Brunswick a few miles from the Kennebec, was that river's most ardent laureate. In poems, essays, novels, and histories, the Bowdoin professor celebrated the river, most vividly in *Kennebec: Cradle of Americans* (1937), the most exuberant chapter being "Kennebec Crystals." Nothing heats the blood of a Maine

---

* When the ice broke up in the spring, ships and barges came alongside the icehouses to load up. Longshoremen set a record loading four hundred tons in a single day. On another day in midsummer of 1880 an observer counted 113 schooners loading ice north of Bath.

writer like a midwinter cold snap blown in from the Arctic on a northwest gale, "good freezing nights for starting the crop of the water." While Coffin was still in grade school, the market monkey-business of voracious monopolists such as Charles Morse of the Knickerbocker Ice Company* had

* Corrupt manipulation of the source and cost of ice aped the machinations of John D. Rockefeller, the robber baron of Standard Oil. Bath's own Charles Morse merged Knickerbocker Ice Company into Consolidated Ice, and Consolidated into the American Ice Company. The mergers in New York were strong-armed by Tammany Hall goons, who vandalized the property and persons of those in the ice business reluctant to be bought out cheap. With a monopoly from Boston to Baltimore, Morse promoted a capitalization of his company at sixty million dollars in 1899. The stock was ludicrously overpriced, even allowing for the revenues to be extorted when the Ice King hiked the price of one hundred pounds of ice from twenty-five to sixty cents less than twenty-four hours after cornering the market in April 1900. He achieved this audacious scandal by bribing Robert A. Van Wyck, the Tammany Hall mayor of New York, and the Tammany Hall dock commissioner, and the Tammany Hall boss (who bore the Dickensian name Richard Croker). The bribe took the form of a gift of many shares in the Ice Securities Corporation, a holding company, following a wintertime visit by the Tammany Hall boys to the icehouses along the Kennebec River as Morse's guests. The New York *World* calculated that Mayor Van Wyck's salary brought him $41.09 per day; his interest in American Ice earned $95 per day. William Randolph Hearst's New York *Journal* stoked the fire of scandal as only Hearst could, with daily applications of kindling, and the paper filed an injunction against Morse's company on May 8, little more than a month following the price hike, "to relieve the poor and suffering from the soulless greed and grip of one of the meanest forms of monopoly." With trust-busting Governor Teddy Roosevelt taking notice, the price eased. Morse's next enterprise was the manipulation of coastal shipping. Finally he was himself shipped to Atlanta, to federal prison, convicted of financial irregularities.

outraged consumers, and the spread of electric refrigeration was quenching the boom forever (the last sea shipment of ice left the Kennebec in 1919), but Coffin had seen a few harvests and heard his family and neighbors tell about the very good and not-so-old days. "Down Hudson, up Kennebec! In the morning, there would be no more waves running on the river. The water looked like a long, dark looking glass dropped between the hills. In a hundred sheds the grindstones were humming." Humming was right: Schools let out so that kids could help their parents mark and cut and haul the ice. The river ice required a thickness of at least a foot, and more reliably fifteen inches. So many hands were demanded during the ice rush that migrant laborers would materialize at the Kennebec immediately following the first cold snap and deep freeze. They hopped freight trains in the later years, or walked the tracks. They'd put up in boardinghouses in Bath, if they could afford it, or—if they couldn't—sleep in icehouses as inviting as an English public school dormitory. From the time they arrived at the river until they left, to walk the ice they wore steel-pronged boots, which were hard on Bath's floors and wooden sidewalks. In "The Harvest of Diamonds," an essay revisiting the ice boom written fifteen years after *Kennebec: Cradle of Americans,* Coffin describes the arrangements: Bedded in huge sheds built by the ice companies, each migrant worker was supplied with a blanket.

A fellow was hired to keep the one woodstove fired through the night. "The other men lay down in windrows in their calked boots." Packed like fish in a can, they were obliged to indulge their restlessness concurrently. "'Break joints!' was the cry, and then men rolled over in unison. The workers slept with their picks, too." The picks, employed to break ice and to save their lives if they broke through, were plenty sharp, but every spring a dozen or so bodies clad in layers of wool and shod in calked boots would pop to the surface near Popham Beach. For the risks they ran these vagrants were paid less than two dollars per day, and of that would give back fifty cents for a bed and three meals. At the tail end of the job chain were boys who followed the horses and swept their turds from the river's surface. And the least shall be best: Without the sweeper's care a Cuban *mojito* chilled by Kennebec ice would have been a less tasty highball.

In addition to the bounty it produced, a thousand tons to the acre, the frozen river made for frolic as well, breaking the tedium of a long Maine winter of isolation and cabin fever. The younger children flocked to the river, skating and playing grab-ass in scenes reminiscent of Pieter Brueghel's—both the Elder's and Younger's— winterscapes (even unto the Younger's depiction of a skater falling through the ice). The Kennebec frozen became a highway, making it easy to visit friends and relatives strung up and down its banks, otherwise accessible only by many miles of snow-covered roads. Sleigh races were arranged. Locals angled through augured holes for smelts; the silvery little fish shoal in huge schools under the ice and a dozen or two taste delicious, bones and all, when fried fresh. Above all they gather talkative friends, in a woodstove-heated shack amply supplied with warming rum.

They enjoyed the sensual beauty of the Kennebec during what Coffin calls those "steel-bright days": the sun glancing off its polished surface, the occasional cannon report of shifting ice plates sounding like cracking thunder, the weight yet magical mobility of ice. The ice also gave an excuse to show off toys designed for recreation but more consequentially those ingenious contraptions invented to reap the greatest harvest of ice from the least hours and effort. Scores of tools were provided for the complex task of getting ice out of a river and out to sea. It had to be surveyed and claimed according to customs as mysterious yet iron-bound as those governing the harvesting of lobsters today. First the river was scraped clean of any blanket of insulating snow. The ice was partitioned into checkerboard patterns by scoring grid lines with a parade of horse-drawn groovers, gouging with a blade progressive cuts of five to twelve inches, and then it was cut by various saws, typically crosscuts with one handle removed. Holes were bored in the river by various augers to bring water atop it, a process to add thickness called "sinking the pond." Picks of various design, "busting bars," were swung to break apart the cakes. These were dragged or pushed along a chiseled canal to the icehouses where contraptions—typically steam-powered engines hoisting the blocks and moving an endless oak-lugged chain—hauled them up a ramp to be planed and skidded and stacked to the rooftops. Working the icehouse was dangerous: Close attention had to be paid to prevent shifts. The slippery cakes, Coffin writes, "had to be humored in handling, for, in spite of their heft, they were fragile as glass and easily broken. The vast cathedral of ice was full of thunder as the ice cakes came running, full of the thunder of men's shouts as they coaxed the cakes into place."

Because of the hazard and difficulty of loading ice, together with its weight and inherent instability, ship captains didn't like to carry it. In the earliest days of the trade, they fretted that the ice would melt and—violating the custom that water is meant to be kept on the outside rather than within the vessel—the ship would sink. Captains and crew also resented being warned by the ice's owners that they'd best keep their hatches sealed. After shrinking ten percent during its storage ashore, the passages by ship—as long as six months to India—caused much more loss, despite enormous quantities of insulation. In a single shipment of two thousand tons of ice to Cuba, two hundred *cords* of wood shavings were put aboard. Yet, wood chips carried boring insects into the hold of a wooden ship,* and flake charcoal, rice, wheat chaff, silicate cotton, and granulated cork—sealed against the skin of the double-hulled ship by sheet zinc to discourage rats—were expensive insulating alternatives. Ice produced great quantities of freshwater melt, and unventilated fresh water trapped in bilges and saturating planks and timbers is a sure formula for the oxymoronically named dry rot.

When electric refrigeration burst the ice bubble, the bonanza died not with a whimper but a bang. The bang was the sound of ice warehouses being burned along the Kennebec for insurance payouts, until no company would insure the buildings. These icehouse fires were spectacular and explosive, stoked by sawdust and burning so quickly that they'd sometimes leave great walls of stacked ice that hadn't had time enough to melt. In 1901, the year following Charles Morse's peculations

---

* Admiral Morison's *Maritime History of Massachusetts* notes that it was assumed that a crew member returning from Calcutta was wise to wear his shoes to bed: "Whoever left his boots outside his bunk (it is said) found nothing in the morning but the nails and the eyelets."

with Tammany Hall, no ice at all was commercially harvested on the Kennebec. Now, as Coffin tells in *Kennebec,* the icehouses that weren't burned "are rotting and falling back into the earth. Their interiors are taken over by the wasps and the mice. The old piers are sinking into the water.... The gouges and saws are rusted away. For the Kennebec crystals, last harvest of Maine's finest river, have joined the white pine and the spruce, the sturgeon and shad and salmon. The end is elegy."

I DON'T THINK SO. SINCE COFFIN WROTE, THE RIVER HAS come alive again. Striped bass abound, dozens of bald eagles are nesting on its banks, sturgeon are again jumping up and down the Kennebec, waterfowl still migrate in their thousands, congregating on Merrymeeting Bay. The Bath Iron Works builds ships; it's the biggest employer in Maine, and when the shifts change the town's streets fill with men and women in hardhats and carrying lunch pails. The local sports bar gets a good turnout, but not so passionately dedicated a clientele as a legendary local roadhouse of previous decades, catering to Bath Iron workers who commuted to the job on Harleys. This tavern kept the local clinics and hospitals busy setting limbs and stitching cuts, taking an awful toll on those BIW employees who expressed opinions about the federal government—or the divinity of Jesus Christ, or the Bruins—contrary to the point of view of the guy on the neighboring stool. So many sick days were lost to bar fights at this roadhouse that the Bath Iron Works bought the place, with the provision that its owner could not open any drinking establishment within an hour's motorcycle ride from the dry dock. Featherbedding has never been a Maine tradition, but local lore has it that when a Navy inspector dropped in on the BIW during World War II to check on the yard's prodigious production of destroyers, he stood on a platform looking down at the beehive of welders and riveters and asked the plant manager, "How many people are working here?" "About half," was the response.

CASTINE (REVISITING)

Eaton's Boatyard

To make do, making a living:

> *to throw away nothing,*
practically nothing, nothing that may
come in handy;

> *within an inertia of caked paintcans,*
frozen C-clamps, blown strips of tarp, and
pulling-boat molds,

> *to be able to find,*
for whatever it's worth,

> *what has to be there:*
the requisite tool

> *in this culch there's no end to:*
the drawshave buried in potwarp,
chain, and manila jibsheets,

                                      or, under a bench,
the piece that already may fit
                                      the idea it begins
to shape up:
                        not to be put off by split rudders,
stripped outboards, half
a gasket, and nailsick garboards:
                                   to forget for good
all the old year's losses,
                              save for
what needs be retrieved:
                                a life given to
how today feels:
                        to make of what's here
what has to be made
to make do.

    —PHILIP BOOTH, *Relations: Selected Poems, 1950–1985*

Kenny Eaton is a character. He's the most recent in a long line of Eatons who have owned and managed Eaton's Boatyard, a great shingled barn jutting from the western shore of Castine's Bagaduce River. Philip Booth's tribute to the Eaton enterprise conveys formally—with its bits and pieces of lines seeming to lie helter-skelter around the poem's floor, hung higgledy-piggledy from the poem's walls and ceiling—the calculated chaos of a business whose archaeological layers are a museum of a community's maritime history. An anchor picked off the beach in 1952 might be sold cheap fifty years later to a sailor who needs just *that* anchor. It's a treat to pick your way through the odds and ends in the huge, dark warehouse, taking not on faith but as verified historical fact that the junk is treasure, such as an old pulling-boat with its transom missing, put up on blocks for Kenny to get to when he has a mind to get to it. In the summer he holds court on the water side of Eaton's, laughing and teasing and drinking with the whole range of Castine citizens and visitors. He is a man of firm opinions volubly expressed. He keeps an eye on the fuel dock and the floats where boats come and go, taking on ice and groceries and water. Be considerate: Don't overstay your welcome, or treat any of Kenny's staff—that's his daughter over there, assigning slip space to transients—high-handedly. Kenny affects rough manners, but don't try rough manners on him or his.

The crew hanging out on Kenny Eaton's dock are Castine's inner circle. You wouldn't mistake the place for a yacht club, though the Castine Yacht Club offers the Eaton Cup as one of its treasured annual racing prizes. For a couple of years we kept *Blackwing* at Eaton's. He put down a mooring for us on the east side of the harbor, hauled our boat in the fall, to hibernate in inside storage through the winter, prepared, rigged, and launched her in the late spring. These labor-intensive acts of preparation and repair took place as though by magic. No formal instructions were demanded—or welcomed—by the proprietor. Yard bills—which, in the fancier-looking venues along the New England coast, resemble hospital bills following major surgery—came late and were poorly itemized and charged at rates that couldn't have increased since I first visited Castine in 1953.

In many other ways the town has not changed in half a century. It is still orderly, a collection of quietly opulent Georgian and federal houses, with an occasional colonial here and there. As you approach the town from Battle Avenue, you pass a pretty public golf course with a modest clubhouse. Turning toward the water, along Main Street, the prospect pleases. You may have noticed—especially if you live in Hummerland, whatever southern California or Connecticut suburban address that may suggest—a paucity of SUVs. You may have noticed leisurely pedestrian traffic along what must be as pretty a Main Street as exists anywhere. You'll see, predictably, a couple of inns, antique stores, real estate offices. And Main Street isn't even the best of it! Water Street, along the campus of the Maine Maritime Academy and Perkins Street out to Dice Head light, has handsome old shingled cottages fronting the harbor. Inland, along Court Street, is a gorgeous common, bordered by houses joined with the care lavished on the 121 tall ships built here in the nineteenth century. Robert Lowell lived in one of those houses and wrote "Skunk Hour" about the experience. Castine is no boutique; it's the real deal prosperous Maine town, soaked in history (and in history's blood).

If not for the bloodshed, the centuries of squabbling over this patch of Maine would resemble a comic opera. The first Europeans to find it were the French, in 1604, guided by Samuel de Champlain. Nine years later the French established a trading post, and the following year John Smith sailed in, noting with dismay the presence of Britain's despised antagonists. In 1626 the Plymouth Colony, in need of quick money, established its own fur-trading post. These colonists were systematically robbed and burned out by the Abnaki and the French. As soon as the Plymouth expedition was driven off in 1635, the French set to quarreling among themselves, the La Tours versus the d'Aulneys. During these times the town and region were known as Pentagöet (by the French) and as Majabagaduce (by the English, who—in the custom of place-naming only—honored the Indian version). Then came from the Basque region of the Pyrenees one Jean-Vincent d'Abbadie de St. Castin, a soldier discharged as a teenager from the French Army in Quebec in 1667, at the conclusion of one of the wars between France and England, settled by the Treaty of Breda. On his way from Quebec to Pentagöet, guided by Abnaki, Castin developed a passionate interest in the culture and language of the Indians. He settled far enough up the Bagaduce to escape the scrutiny of such missionaries as Brother Leo of Paris, who had established a mission in Pentagöet in 1648. The young gentleman's interest in the natives was regarded as unwholesome by local holy men, and Castin was arrested and pent up in Pentagöet for a couple of months owing, as he explained to the governor of Canada, to "a little weakness I had for some women." He rescued the honor of one of these women by marrying Mathilde, daughter of Madockawando, a sagamore of the Tarratines. Happily ever after with an Indian princess? Not quite. Here came the Dutch, attacking Fort Pentagöet twice, once in 1674 from the sea and then, two years later, coming ashore and turning the fort's defensive cannon on the town. They couldn't hold the fort, however, and the French regained it and held it until the British retook it in 1759. Settlers moved in, declared their independence in 1776, and held on (with the exception of some Loyalists, who had to move out, floating their houses to Canada) until 1779, when the British retook it. The Americans sent an expeditionary force from Massachusetts to kick the Brits out, and in the worst naval defeat of our country's history, the English feinted and counterattacked, driving eighteen armed vessels and a thousand recruits up the Penobscot River, trapping them just about at Norumbega, where Commodore Dudley Saltonstall and Colonel Paul Revere—both of whom were subsequently court-martialed—scuttled the fleet. Never mind: America wouldn't be America if we hadn't regained control of Castine. Remain in your seats; this lesson is not finished. We still have to cover the War of 1812, when the British occupied Castine until 1815.

This story is told in what must be the busiest roadside plaque I've ever read, one of more than a hundred along the byways of Castine, many contradictory and all arguing a particular point of view. You'll find this one on Perkins Street and, please, no skipping:

FORT PENTAGOET

Originally a trading post built during the Winter of 1613—by **SIEUR CLAUDE DE TURGIS DE LA TOUR**

It became, with its accessions, through *nine change of regime* and of successive but continuous occupation the first *permanent settlement* in **NEW ENGLAND** and its actual **POLITICAL & COMMERCIAL BEGINNING**

Captured and rebuilt by **SIR DAVID**

KIRK in 1628—transferred by **GRANT** to the **PLYMOUTH** Colony in 1629—and restored to **FRANCE** by Treaty of St Germain and by force of arms in 1635—it was entirely reconstructed 1636–1645 by **SIEUR CHARLES DE MENOU D'AULNAY DE CHARNIZAY** who made it one of the **LARGEST** and Most **FORMIDABLE FORTIFICATIONS** in the **NEW WORLD**.

Named by him **FORT SAINT PETER** and by the English the **PNOBSCOT FORT**—under the Dominion of FRANCE—1613-28—1635-54—1670-74—1676-1745 ◇ of **ENGLAND** 1628-35—1654-70 and of the **UNITED NETHERLANDS** 1674-76.

It became the **SEAT** of **GOVERNMENT** for **ACADIA** in 1670 and four years later of the Province **NEWHOLLANDIA**, the capture of which by **BARON DE ST. CASTIN**—Nov. 1676, ended **DUTCH** authority in **AMERICA**.

It was five times carried by assault—twice surrendered by royal decree and once by Treaty of Breda—twice raided—once unsuccessfully besieged—once invested and its truck house plundered by three-hundred

Mohawks in 1662—and once partially and once completely destroyed.

Rebuilt much smaller in 1677 by **BARON JEAN VINCENT D'ABADDIE DE SAINT CASTIN** and thenceforth known as **CASTIN'S FORT**—It was again raided by Sir Edmund Andros in 1688 and by Col. Benjamin Church in 1704—and was finally **DEMOLISHED** by Castin's sons in 1745 to prevent its coming under English control, Possession of the locality thus retained until 1760.

During the One hundred and thirty-one years of its existence, its Strength, Strategic position and Enormous Revenues commanded constant Old and New World recognition as factors always to be Reckoned With in Inter-Colonial political and commercial affairs.

Its story is the most varied and dramatic of any American Fortress of its time.*

---

*Nearby is set a more minimalist plaque, noting: BURIAL PLACE OF FIVE DUTCH SEAMEN AND THREE FRENCH SOLDIERS KILLED DURING THE ENGAGEMENT AUGUST 10, 1674. A roadside marker in Bar Harbor declares, ON THIS SITE IN 1897 NOTHING HAPPENED. But the Bert 'n' I silver cup for taciturnity goes to a hand-lettered roadside sign I saw east of Schoodic claiming: NOTHING HAPPENED AROUND HERE. EVER. Honorary mention surely is due the American Legion's Smith Tobey Post in Bath, whose front-lawn sign—the kind found in front of churches, quoting scripture, and announcing next Sunday's sermon—asked the runic question: IF A MAN ALONE AT SEA SPEAKS WHILE HIS WIFE IS ASHORE, IS HE STILL WRONG?

During the two summers Priscilla and I spent in Castine we'd often walk past that marker and study it, and give each other snap quizzes on its names and sequences, and essay questions touching the partisan subtext of its narrative. We rented a cabin on the Penobscot River and a boathouse perched on a dock in front of the Castine Harbor Lodge. Our favorite dwelling was loaned to us by our daughter-in-law and her family, their house on Water Street across the street from the Castine Variety Store, which sells ... well, a variety of things: the *New York Times* and notions 'n' lotions and fishing lures and the best crab rolls ever. Living in that house, in the red-hot center of town, made us honorary citizens of the town. My daughter-in-law's grandparents, Minnie and Ivan Nelson, had inherited the house from Minnie's aunt, Mrs. MacLeod, who had run a year-round sandwich shop and soda fountain next door to her house, Ma MacLeod's, an attraction much favored by the students at Maine Maritime Academy. Ivan Nelson loved boats. Minnie believed boats to be damned foolishness, and told her husband so, and if he even suggested that he might like to own a boat, the hammer came right down on him: "You'll just get yourself drowned!" So he'd wander over to Eaton's Boatyard to watch Kenny assemble an outboard motor that had only yesterday been a random scatter of parts in a carton, or to see Kenny clamber up the mast in a bosun's chair to rewire an antenna. He would help Kenny or Kenny's dad with projects on the water, such as moving boats from their slips to moorings when weather threatened trouble; taking boats over to the Penobscot River to bring them home in the spring; putting moorings down or pulling them.

There's an art to moving reinforced concrete fixed to a length of sturdy chain, the gear together weighing as much as two tons. The huge blocks need to be placed on a piece of the bottom precisely chosen to allow sufficient swing room for adjacent boats—moved inconsistently by wind or current—to lie at any conceivable angle to one another without hitting, yet not so distant from one another to waste precious mooring space. Some boatyards use a barge equipped with a crane to manipulate moorings; Eaton's relied on *Annabelle,* a swift powerboat built in 1934 for a rusticator to ferry himself and his family from Mount Desert to Cranberry Island. Thirty-five feet, with a top speed of thirty knots, *Annabelle* was bought by the Eaton family in 1967 for nine hundred dollars. They put in a new engine and the yard used her as a towboat and, off-season, Kenny used her to drag for scallops, an enterprise notoriously hard on fishermen, gear, and boats. Equipped with a sturdy boom, *Annabelle* set and pulled and moved the yard's many moorings; she has a black hull with a white pilothouse, a gold cove stripe, and gold lightning flashes at her bow. Kenny has been heard to declare, "You ain't got money enough to buy her."

And that was *after* she sank at her own mooring in 1997, in sixty feet of water. The strain of all that work over all those years had loosened *Annabelle*'s planks and transom, and her bilge pumps couldn't keep pace with the leaks. You might think it was time to call the insurance agent. Instead, Kenny sent a diver down to attach a hawser to *Annabelle*'s bow bit, and towed her, submerged, at highest tide as close to the beach as he could get her. As told by Captain Jim Moorhead, when the tide ebbed *Annabelle* sat high and dry, resting on her beam. "Kenny then put a few [support] stands on her high side, ran a line from the top of her mast to his pickup truck, pulled her upright, and put stands on the opposite side." Before the tide flooded six hours later he had patched her up enough to float. "He changed the oil, plugs, and distributor cap, fired her up, and went to work."

Kenny Eaton's ingenuity is legendary among local boat owners. He is as undaunted by hopeless cases as are those mechanics in Cuba who keep 1948 DeSotos and 1949 Hudson Hornets purring. So his solutions are especially in demand by owners of vintage sailboats. One such owner, a new-minted captain of industry with a summer mansion commanding the heights of Islesboro, a short sail from Castine, ran up a goodly yard bill at Eaton's. The bill, slowly delivered, was even more tardily paid. It mounted. Kenny sent reminders. I'd call them "gentle reminders," but I know better. (Kenny calls a lot of people "dear," a Maine honorific pronounced DEE-uh and used, in the description of folklorist Edgar Alex Been, "dispassionately to address anyone, regardless of age or gender.") It is difficult to get money on Kenny's mind, but I think that once it gets there it stays there. And it's no trick at all to get his dander up. So this was how it happened that—during an Independence Day lawn party at the vintage boat owner's summer retreat, croquet mallets and wickets in place, ladies in sun dresses and gents in white flannels—here came a helicopter, piloted by a friend of Kenny's, and out of that bird stepped Kenny, wearing boatyard clothes and holding in his hand a bill. Mr. Eaton did not have to wait very long at all to have that bill paid in full.

ELEGIES, HAIRBREADTH ESCAPES, AND REPAIRS

The yellow leavings of the logs poured into the river year by year, covering over the rich dark feeding grounds of salmon and trout, killing the fry, carpeting the {Kennebec} with a carpet of death. The March floods scoured the sawdust out in places, but there was always more sawdust to come.... The paper mills of Augusta and Gardiner did for the water above the carpet of sawdust and bark. They ate up Maine's wealth in young trees and spewed out their venom and acids.

—ROBERT P. TRISTRAM COFFIN, *Kennebec: Cradle of Americans* (1937, revised 1965)

It was the growth of the pulp industry that ruined the Kennebec as anything but a working river. A

river should be beautiful—and the Kennebec is still
that—and useful, which the Kennebec has always
been. But in addition, it should be a source of pleas-
ure, which the Kennebec is no longer. The sawdust
from the mills has covered the feeding grounds of the
fish, and the chemicals used in the manufacture of
paper have polluted and poisoned the water. There's
no more good fishing except way up near the head-
waters, and nobody in his right mind would think
of swimming in the dirty water. It's too bad.
— LOUISE RICH, *The Coast of Maine* (1956)

There's no end to elegies, of course, and no surprise.
After all, this twenty-five-hundred miles of jagged
coastline, a drowned mountain range scoured and
crushed and ground by glaciers, underwent what geolo-
gists term a prehistoric "ordeal." But in such a setting,
so primal and extreme, happened upon by explorers
awed by its staggering bounty, the place must have
seemed indestructible. Settlers and their progeny clear-
cut the virgin hardwoods and then the evergreens. They
killed off the wolves and ate the eggs of puffins. They
shot seals because the seals competed for the plentiful
fish. Then they fished the fish damned near out of existence. They trapped otters on the riverbanks and beaver
from their dams. Then they built their own dams to

harness the river's energy, and incidentally put paid to the alewife runs and shad runs and salmon runs. They poured their shit into the rivers, and then they invented chemical shit to finish the job. Impacted sawdust and junk flotsam so choked the channels of the Penobscot and Kennebec that river traffic jammed to a halt. The comeoverers and their successors bought cheap from the Abnaki and then sold cheap to the rusticators and hotel owners. It's the oldest story in the books, and as Louise Rich notes, it sure is too bad.

Except here I am living on the Kennebec River, and I'm in my right mind. I swim in the river a mile north of Bath, and so do sturgeon and striped bass. We see eagles every day. A few years ago, just after we bought our house, I got a letter from a friend with whom I've sailed forty years, and many days in Maine. He spent his boyhood and adolescent summers just east of Camden, on Ducktrap Cove in Lincolnville, and he built a house on Vinalhaven overlooking Hurricane Island. Much of what I first experienced in Maine I learned from him. He's a taciturn fellow, with a dry sense of humor, and when I boasted of setting down shallow roots on the Kennebec I didn't expect him to go sentimental on me, to break a bottle of Mumm's over the doorsill. But what I got in place of congratulations was a clear-eyed report about what Bath might have become. Until it was dismantled this past summer, the Maine Yankee nuclear facility was one river over and a few miles east by road in Wiscasset, the "prettiest village in Maine" (measured by its own aesthetic standards), the "worm capital of Maine" (measured by its impact on the live-bait business), and site of legendary traffic jams on Route 1 (owing to its pedestrians' sullen, leisurely insistence on availing themselves of the right-of-way in several crosswalks on the town's main drag). My friend reminded me that Maine Yankee and the Bath Iron Works were likely targets of al Qaeda and still "ground zero for some old 3M25 Scorpion class nuclear-tipped missiles now under the supervision of Uzbeki rebels who don't know how to retarget them and figure, what the hell, let's light them off and see where they go." He neglected to mention Brunswick Naval Air Station, a few miles south, center for anti-submarine warfare during the Cold War and currently the second largest employer in Maine. Continuing his assessment of my real estate investment, my dear friend wrote that "as far as the waterfront aspects are concerned, surely you must never have visited the place at low water springs, when the sulphurous mud flats combined with the PCBs dumped up there in the sixties, creates an air quality to which no decent grandfather would ever expose an heir. Of course you might ask, 'an heir to what?' Good point." He closed by assuring me that in

Bath I should be able to find retail outlets for numerous manufacturers of Hazmat gear. "These protective costumes have the added merit of keeping more or less at bay the swallow-sized mosquitoes."

In fact, the mosquitoes aren't so bad on our patch along the river. Maybe the cardinals and chickadees eat them, maybe the eagles and ospreys scare them off, but we endure. My old friend must be referring to Vinalhaven, infamous breeding ground of the Maine state bird. And Ducktrap Cove: I remember a Memorial Day week we spent there in 1970 when we hid in his driveway, cowering in our car from the black flies that would carry us away if we made a run for his parents' casually screened house. Polluters didn't bring bugs, but they nearly killed off the eagles and ospreys trying to get rid of them. And if DDT had done its work to the very end, the mosquito-less Maine coast would be infested with rusticators, and Fox Island Thorofare might look like Myrtle Beach, with miniature golf courses, a roller coaster, and cotton candy stands. If there's such a vice as an attractive nuisance, there's such a virtue as a repellent nuisance. In the seventeenth century, John Josselyn noticed the pests:

> *The Country is strangely incommodated with flies,*
> *which the English call Musketaes, they are like our*

*gnats, they will sting so fiercely in summer as to
make the faces of the English swell'd and scabby, as
if the small pox for the first year. Likewise there is
a small black fly no bigger than a flea, so numerous
up in the Country, that a man cannot draw his
breath, but he will suck of them in: they continue
about Thirty days say some but I say three months,
and are not only a pesterment but a plague to the
Country. There is another sort of fly called a
Gurnipper, that are like our horse-flyes, and will
bite desperately, making the blood to spurt out in
great quantity.*

The disincentive to rusticators of biting insects may
seem petty—an instance of what Albert Camus termed
the "fleas of life"—but the pollution of the Maine coast
might have been calamitous. Belfast, one of the Maine
coast's most economically and culturally prosperous
cities—where a governor chose to build his mansion and
shipbuilders and whaling captains settled during the
nineteenth century—was a sick joke when I first cruised
Penobscot Bay in the late 1960s. After the town's busy
docks fell into desuetude and ruin, a sardine processing
plant on Belfast Bay gave way to a couple of huge chick-
en processors. The bay turned bloodred, and gizzards
floated on the surface. "When you sailed up Belfast Bay

on the swan-crested waves," advised Don Johnson's *Cruising Guide to Maine,* "it was neither sea-foam on the crests, nor was it swan feathers." You wouldn't expect a depressed community to recover from such a decline, and when the poultry processors left for the South, Belfast might have slipped into terminal decay. But that's not what happened. MBNA, the credit card company, came to an unlikely rescue, and Belfast is now an ace attraction of the coast. What drew MBNA to Maine was what drew many businesses to Ireland: a well-educated population of underemployed citizens with a cosmopolitan history of shipping out and a rooted history of staying put. It didn't hurt that the state—with its tradition of lumbering, farming, fishing, and shipbuilding—had a legendary work ethic. MBNA first wooed Belfast—promising and delivering on their promise to fund libraries, harbor cleanup, architectural restoration, college scholarships—and then won it. It built a credit card processing facility—the place you get when you phone 1-800-COMPLAIN—and hired fifteen hundred local workers.

It is the kind of initiative that Joshua Lawrence Chamberlain, a three-term governor of the state during the late 1860s and early 1870s, wanted so desperately for the state and despaired of ever attaining. Chamberlain was Maine's great moral and intellectual hero, the Civil

War general who won the Congressional Medal of Honor and took Lee's surrender at Appomattox. He taught at Bowdoin—as a faculty member and president—every subject in the college's curriculum save math and physics. Well he understood his natal state's perilous dependence on perishable natural resources. "What this state needs is capital, money in motion" he said at his 1870 inauguration. "Our material is stagnant, our industry crippled, our enterprise staggered for want of money, which is power."

The principal means of escape from the area's serial economic depressions has always been the quick fix of creating energy—Maine Yankee followed a long history of damming Maine's historic rivers—or running the risks of refining and conveying oil and gas. The cover story in the June 2001 issue of *Down East* magazine is titled "What If?" It should have been published on Halloween; it's a scary story of a horror show that didn't happen. The magazine selected ten watershed votes and decisions that turned Maine's course as consequentially as turning an oil tanker on a collision course with a reef. Two catastrophes averted were dams. The Dickey-Lincoln Dam along the St. John River, to be built by the U.S. Army Corps of Engineers, would have despoiled that river's wildness. The hydroelectric project would have created a recreational lake of 134 square miles, aimed to encourage motorized water sports and RV camping. This project was killed by the U.S. Congress in 1982. At about the same time Great Northern Paper Company proposed building a hydroelectric plant and dam—known by friends and foes as the Big A—at Big Amberjackmockamus Falls, on the West Branch of the Penobscot and a few miles from Millinocket, the company's headquarters. Environmentalists rated that site the "most significant stretch of river in Maine," a world-class white-water run. For this and other reasons a coalition led by the Natural Resources Defense Council of Maine fought Great Northern remorselessly, and so pestered the huge, influential company that it threw up its hands in disgust and quit the field. As *Down East* is scrupulous to report, having Great Northern take its business elsewhere was good for Maine, but it was mighty hard on those Mainers who lost their jobs, sending Millinocket into a "downward economic spiral that has not yet bottomed out." The giant company, Maine's greatest landowner, sold out and broke up the pieces; the population of Millinocket has declined since the defeat of the Big A by one-quarter; fourteen hundred jobs were lost and have stayed lost.

Down East frames the counter-conservation argument colloquially: "You can't eat the scenery," "It's pickerel or payrolls," "My kids are more important than your trees." In these matters the long view seems almost always to be the better view, but in the short run losing a job or a decent tax base is pretty much without consolation. Some of the ten rescues listed by *Down East* had a slight and maybe even nonexistent downside: Maine's anti-billboard law, hard-fought and hard-won, resulted in the dismantling between 1969 and 1984 of eighty-five-hundred roadside signs as egregious as any in the nation, eyesores competing with one another for garishness and scale. Who's the poorer, other than the outdoor advertising business? Shame on me, but about them I feel as I do about telemarketers and spammers who lose their source of income when regulation constricts their mischief.

The rescues along the Maine coast are unambiguous victories. The scariest of them all was a proposal in the 1970s to build in Eastport an oil refinery and supertanker port. The company who made the proposal was Pittston, a Virginia-based coal business named for the town in Pennsylvania, set between Scranton and Wilkes-Barre, in a blighted pocket mining anthracite unto its final feeble vein, until the 1959 Knox Mine disaster in next-door Port Griffith put an effective end to that particular exploitation. "Eastport was a depressed, economically battered little city ... that had two things Pittston needed: deepwater access for huge supertankers and local officials eager for new jobs and industry." Passamaquoddy Bay and the waters on the approaches to Eastport have other qualities as well: They are fogbound, with narrow tide-ripped passages through cuts of granite teeth. An oil spill—so incontestably likely that even while the project was being pitched it was a *when* rather than an *if*—would have propelled millions of tons of crude, driven by ferocious tides, up and down the fecund, wild coast. The scheme was finally killed in 1979 by the Environmental Protection Agency, which refused to grant a permit to proceed because the projected refinery would threaten bald eagles and their aeries.

That the eagles were there at all to prevent the Pittston refinery is owing to another of *Down East*'s celebrated rescues. This stemmed from the creation of a Board of Pesticide Control, created by the state legislature in the immediate back draft of Rachel Carson's *Silent Spring* and left unfunded until 1970, when its persuasive chief persuaded blueberry and potato farmers, not to mention citizens attached to the custom of outdoor grilling, that there were even worse things in their world than potato bugs and mosquitoes, and even if there weren't, DDT sprayed from airplanes was not the most rational means to attack them. The Maine Board of Pesticide Control saved Maine's raptors (together, I guess, with Maine's mosquitoes).

Since Eastport couldn't have its tanker port and refinery, how about Sanford, eighteen miles west of the Bush cottage in Kennebunkport? "Sanford was once the model of a modern New England mill town, but, as the factories closed and moved south, the city had slipped deep into economic doldrums. The new refinery, which would have exceeded the combined output of all six refineries then operating in New Jersey, promised hundreds of jobs." Let's pause here just a sec. Have you ever driven the New Jersey Turnpike south from the Lincoln Tunnel or George Washington Bridge? Sure you have. If you're a writer you've probably written about it, everybody's favorite valley of ashes, where Tony Soprano has bodies planted and fiery smokestacks spew toxic fumes. The Gibbs Oil Company, whose bright idea this was, meant to pipe the crude from the Portland waterfront to Sanford and then pipe back the unrefined waste and dump it into Casco Bay by way of the Fore River. That would be the Fore River where an Audubon Bird Sanctuary is now located, just about where the pipes would have been laid. This craziness was beaten back by coalitions of York County residents—natives and newcomers in harness together—and by organic gardeners and environmentalists who have learned that if the law is, as Dickens tells us, an ass, why not ride it through meadows, while breathing fresh air?

THE RAISING AND RAZING OF MAINE YANKEE ATOMIC Power Station is an exemplary Maine progression. Out of nearby Wiscasset's sight but within the town's boundaries, the facility began doing its thing to uranium atoms in 1972, heating water to become steam to run turbines and generate electricity. And money, of course. Colin Woodard, author most recently of *The Lobster Coast* (2004), has made himself an authority on Maine Yankee's bumpy story. Writing for the *Bulletin of the Atomic Scientists* in 1997, Woodard explained that the facility generated 20 percent of Maine's energy needs and 90 percent of Wiscasset's town taxes. Who could complain? The facility seemed to have a Midas touch, bringing to reality the dream of perpetual motion and the philosopher's stone. It replaced a coal-fired (and later oil-fired) power plant; who missed the ashes and smoke? The electricity nuclear power generated would soon be "too cheap to meter," the boosters promised. A Wiscasset selectman remembered that she grew up referring to Maine Yankee as the "golden goose." Wiscasset spent ten thousand dollars apiece on its students and treated itself to shiny new fire trucks. The only burr under the town's saddle was a nagging question asked by a few bitter-end doom-and-gloomers: What was going to be done with the spent fuel? Then came 1979, Three Mile Island.

As Woodard—then in grammar school—writes: "Our television screens showed thousands of kids my age being evacuated from their Pennsylvania homes and dosed with iodine in emergency clinics." Three Mile Island grabbed the attention of seaside residents who had isolated themselves out on the tips of the fingers made by the many rivers in the area—the Kennebec and Sheepscot and Damariscotta—who would have to evacuate along a very few narrow, twisting roads leading to Route 1, jammed at the best of times and very near which Maine Yankee perched. Had the sirens screamed, "nothing short of a wide-scale evacuation by sea could have saved all those people," as a state senator and resident of Boothbay Harbor told Woodard. Neighboring townspeople turned against the plant. Farmers had their cows' milk examined for contamination, and some didn't like the test results. In 1997, Maine Yankee made the Nuclear Regulatory Commission's list of worst-run nuclear plants in the nation. Steam tubes developed cracks. Whistle-blowers warned of maintenance shortcuts, chronic regulatory violations. Forced shutdowns followed; emergency shutdowns doomed the enterprise. Referenda to close it down began. Meantime, the friends and families of those who worked at Maine Yankee were not without their own interest, and Woodard tells that there began to appear in the neighborhood T-shirts with the legend "Keep Nuclear Power in Maine," above the afterthought, "A Little 'Nukie' Never Hurt Anybody." Uh-oh. There went half the vote. The power plant was taken offline in 1997, and the dome itself was demolished September 2004. Left behind are more than a thousand spent fuel assemblies, almost nine hundred tons of radioactive waste unfit for human handling for the next thousand centuries. Until someone figures out how to get them to Yucca Flats, if Yucca Flats will take them, those isotopes are buried right there on the Back River, and Wiscasset's property owners will pay taxes double and triple what they had paid comparable to taxes along the rest of the Maine coast.

Wise people, conservationists and environmental scientists among them, regret the fate of Maine Yankee, or at least the end of rational discussion of the benefits and risks of nuclear generation of power. Maine is stuck downwind from the toxic clouds that rain acidly on the state from coal- and oil-fired industries to its west. Clean power is in Maine's interest, but not until someone puzzles out how to dispose of the waste. It has been observed that what was built in 1972 was as far-sighted as building a hundred-room hotel without planning a septic system.

SHORTSIGHTEDNESS IS NO LONGER CHARACTERISTIC of Maine's public policies and private initiatives. The state's voters and rusticators have combined in recent years, in fund drive after ballot initiative after bond issue, to enhance the state's resources. Every edition of a local paper seems to bring news of another rescue. An item in the Brunswick *Times Record* notes the purchase during the summer of 2004 of an eighty-five-acre parcel of wetlands along Whiskeag Creek by the Lower Kennebec Regional Land Trust. This parcel is a small but vital piece of the jigsaw puzzle of stops along the Atlantic flyway, and the payment of $130,000 was itself pieced together by small donations and bequests. Another recent item notes the rescue of the south end of bucolic Barters Island. A subdivision of 128 acres was nearly under way when the Coastal Maine Botanical Gardens, a nonprofit, bought the parcel with the intention of creating, as they promised, "the finest public garden north of Boston."

In 2000, *Down East* acknowledged as a "watershed event" the passage of a fifty-million-dollar bond issue to underwrite the state's purchase of land threatened by developers. This referendum was offered in 1999, during an off-year election, and stirred much greater interest than referendum questions on abortion and medical marijuana.* Of the 410,000 who voted, 69 percent approved the initiative. This was the "largest bond issue ever approved by Maine that didn't underwrite new highways. Moreover, the question passed in every county, north and south. The vote laid to rest any accusation that public-land conservation is a concern only of southern Maine suburbanites who want weekend playgrounds in the North Woods. In fact, the balloting undercut all the tortured theorizing about the so-called Two Maines."

This view may be excessively rosy. Local friction between boosters of new jobs and defenders of old seascapes continues to abrade coastal communities. During the spring of 2004, citizens of Harpswell—a long, lovely peninsula jutting into Casco Bay—debated whether to approve a $350,000,000 liquified natural gas terminal to be erected on their rocky shore. An inevitable collision occurred between summer residents and underemployed year-rounders who were having difficulty paying property taxes inflated by the value to

* On the op-ed page of the *New York Times* of November 20, 2004, the president of the Trust for Public Land, a national conservation organization, notes that unremarked among postmortems of the Bush-Kerry contest was the triumph among voters of all parties of ballot measures calling for taxpayers to spend their money buying local land in order to conserve it. "Of 161 conservation ballot measures, 120—or 75 percent—were approved." (Will Rogers, p. A31)

summer residents of waterfront property. Harpswell has 4,600 voters, and most summer residents aren't included in that number, so the rusticators' campaigns against the erection of the terminal had little consequence, other than to stir the pot of controversy. And that pot came to a boil when Harpswell's lobstermen, fearing pollution of their rich territories and anxious about the cost to safeguard the plant from terrorists and natural disasters and industrial screwups, turned against the proposal. In opposing it, they were rejecting the offer by the energy companies of eight million dollars a year in tax money. The debate grew bitter, with handmade signs and posters simplifying the complicated issues by sloganized insults and denunciations. Family members quarreled with one another and canceled Thanksgiving and Christmas reunion dinners. The morning of the townie vote in March, someone—in an attempt to cancel it— phoned the Harpswell police with a bomb threat. The vote was held and the measure defeated, but bitterness lingers. "It won't be forgotten; it's too deep," a lobsterman told the *Boston Globe*'s Jenna Russell. He had been hauling traps in Harpswell for sixty-two years, and predicted that if one of his neighbors "says something the wrong way, it's going to bring it out again." A woman who supported the plant, and whose husband's family had lived in Harpswell since 1650, complained that fishermen wouldn't speak to her, "wouldn't even wave." Neighbors accused one another of making threats, of lying, of being greedy and/or stupid. A representative of one group, asked whether it was possible to put the dispute behind them, said, "It's their responsibility to apologize." The pronoun reference is ambiguous.

Recent immigrants to Maine, from the professional classes, can be demanding. In 1999, near the site of Belfast's bygone poultry factories, residents complained to state officials that their tranquility was being disturbed by excessive noise produced by idling refrigerator trucks waiting to load potatoes from Penobscot Frozen Foods. Testing revealed the decibel level at the now-bankrupt company's property line to be less than sixty-five decibels, ten decibels under the permitted maximum. The *Bangor Daily News* reported the story with what it must have taken to be objectivity: "Fifteen years ago, when a chicken-processing plant [produced] offensive odors, the neighborhood was made up of working class folk who complained less; now, the neighborhood consists of more wealthy homeowners who have registered increasing number of complaints."

Islands in private hands have made for strains and outright provocations between their owners and the putative public interest. Hog Island, an Audubon bird sanctuary in Muscongus Bay popular with visiting boaters, asked that future editions of the Tafts' *Cruising Guide to the Maine Coast* delete their description of the undeniable fact of the island's geographical presence. "Perhaps Hog Island is just too beautiful," an update to the guide noted. I remember rowing ashore at Butter Island in 1970 from a sailboat we had chartered out of Blue Hill. The island, owned by the Cabots, is as pretty as they come, with meadows and blueberry patches and commanding views from Montserrat Hill of Deer Isle, Islesboro, and North Haven. One of its principal attractions was solitude, and that is what had induced the Outward Bound school over at Hurricane Island to maroon one of its students there for a couple of days. He was meant to scrounge his food from the vegetation at hand, and—when he wasn't gathering victuals—to contemplate the isolation of a single human being dwarfed by the grandeur of the universe. When we came upon the teenager, sitting cross-legged on the island's Nubble Beach, he looked hungry and forlorn; he seemed at once hostile and resigned to companionship. A parade of cruisers such as ourselves had established a beachhead during the past two days to experience the quiet of the island, and as they had come ashore they had caught the boy up in their conversations and helped themselves to the blueberries he had collected and stored at his side in his Red Sox cap. He requested, politely, that we leave him and his blueberries to himself, but not before conceding that the skipper of a handsome Concordia yawl had replaced a handful of berries with a crisp dollar bill. The Cabot family, whose patriarch Tom had a farsighted and benign appetite for Maine islands, which he bought (forty of them by the time he died at ninety-eight) and shared with sailors similarly attracted, recently shut the circus down. The tipping point came a couple of years ago when his grandson, calling in on Butter one summer evening, counted more than 150 visitors crowding its beaches and trails. Three windjammers lay offshore, giving their paying customers lobster bakes on the beach. The Cabots' sight of that herd closed the door to all commercial traffic and restricted access to everyone except invited guests to most of Butter Island. The family distributed a public notice: "This overwhelming number of people has had a negative impact on everyone's island experience. We are also concerned about the long-term ecological health of the island.... We apologize to all those who have been visiting Butter Island for years and can now no longer hike the entire island, but we had no alternative."

Fact is, to think of any of Maine's three thousand or so actual islands as off-limits to the public is to practice sentimental nostalgia. It's true that islands are fragile, that it's easy to kill the lichens by trampling them. The soil is too thin to bury human waste, and let's stipulate that the troglodytes who dump garbage and cut branches or even trees to use as firewood are evildoers. But the islands of the Maine coast have been used from the earliest days of the aborigines: as fishing stations, hunting grounds, granite quarries, and beach-party sites. The state owns fourteen hundred of these islands, and is buying more all the time. This is a good thing.

But for my money the best rescue in Maine has been the deliberate breaching and demolition in 1999 of the Edwards Dam in Augusta. The cribwork dam blocking the Kennebec was built of stones in 1837, a thousand feet across, flooding and stilling fish-rich rapids and falls all the way up to Waterville, seventeen miles away. Opening the floodgates drained the dead water; what happened next astonished even the most optimistic of the dam's enemies.

But first a word about the dam's friends and protectors. Built to provide mechanical power to riverside mills, in 1913 the first of what would be five turbines was installed to produce electric power, used initially by Edwards Mill, but after the bankruptcy of that and so many other Maine textile mills, the dam supplied electricity to Augusta, and not much of it, and at an awful price to birds and spawning fish. Even after the Federal Energy Regulatory Commission declared that Edwards didn't produce enough electricity to justify its cost in environmental damage, many locals warned against breaching it, foretelling that the river would fall ten feet, eroding its banks and exposing the toxins impounded on the dead water's bottom and creating a god-awful sulphurous stink.

None of these side effects occurred. Moreover, the demolition and cleanup created jobs. Ice-fishing outfitters and bass guides were back in business. Almost immediately after Edwards was breached, grass and wildflowers grew from the mud along the Kennebec; paid workers and volunteers hauled away the accumulated litter of pulp logs and truck tires that had been exposed. Aquatic insects came back immediately, followed by the little fish that eat them, followed by the big fish that eat *them*. Here came the birds: eagles and egrets, herons and ospreys and cormorants and even peregrine falcons. Make way for seals and otters and muskrat. All this in five years!

A mile or more up the Kennebec from my house in Bath, just above Lines Island and The Chops, we enter the shallow water of Merrymeeting Bay, a drainage of the watersheds of six rivers, of which the Kennebec is the largest. Because its fresh water is churned by tidal action, fed by fertile currents, the bay's abundance was once upon a time extravagant. The thriving crop of wild rice attracted huge congregations of wildfowl. While Edwards Dam stood, by the 1970s Merrymeeting Bay—one of the richest flyways and fishing grounds in New England—was declared dead, terminally polluted by industrial excess, so starved of dissolved oxygen that everything in and on its turbid water had suffocated. Scummy and stinking, the nine-thousand-acre bay came to be referred to casually as a "cesspool"; it repelled even the old-timers who remembered its glory days, when it was alive with striped bass, alewives, Atlantic sturgeon, smelts, shad, salmon, eels, and who knew what more?

I'll take the horror stories on faith, but when I run my Boston Whaler up the river to Augusta I can hardly believe that the Kennebec and Merrymeeting Bay were ever less than teeming with irresistible life and plenty. We never fail to see eagles, and all summer the sturgeon jump, most of them shortnose but now and again Atlantic sturgeon, the grandest sea-run fish in eastern North America, twelve feet long and weighing up to eight hundred pounds. Other than a few fish remaining in the Delaware and Hudson Rivers, the Atlantic sturgeon in the Kennebec are the species' final stand against extinction, and the news is getting better. (Should a sturgeon—driving from the muddy bottom to the surface and going airborne—chance to land on your dock or in your canoe, better put it back pronto, or pay a five-thousand-dollar fine. That's fine caviar running upstream again.) After Edwards Dam went down, brown trout and blueback herring came again to the river. Atlantic salmon rebounded, and we see them jump now and again in the tributaries below Augusta. Owing to its great freshwater tidal estuary, Merrymeeting Bay has the only spawning population of striped bass in New England. The record catch in the Kennebec was sixty-seven pounds, but now the really big ones and little ones are put back. Striped bass fishing for sport is again booming on the Kennebec, and getting better all the time. Edwards Dam and those above on the Kennebec almost finished off American shad; the river used to host a run of a million or more shad, which spawned in June. The final word isn't in yet on the river's shad recovery. Alewife runs in May and June—landmark events in Abnaki culture—once numbered six million and more of the foot-long adults, prized also by eagles and great blue heron. These staples on the food chain were nearly goners, but they're back, running a million or so.

Franklin Burroughs, one of the best nature essayists—in a line that goes back to John Josselyn and Thoreau, unto Edward Abbey, John McPhee, and Edward Hoagland—grew up on the rivers of South Carolina, with a special fondness for the Waccamaw. He came to Maine many years ago to teach English at Bowdoin College and fell in love with Merrymeeting Bay, where he lives. The banks of the bay remain sparsely developed; perhaps the toxic stink of the bad old days was an effective deterrent to developers. The bay is dotted with little islands and medium-size islands. Population centers tend to be old-fashioned summer camps for kids. Meadows, bound by stone walls and interrupted by woodlots, checkerboard the shore. Vistas shift quickly, and parts of the bay are as perplexing as a maze: That deep-looking river or inlet over there will dry out at low tide, revealing a sandbar or mudflat growing yellow and pale-green grass. Other than the flop of jumping fish or of a seal sliding off a rock into the water, other than the indignant call of an osprey pissed off that some thieving bandito of a cheep-cheeping eagle has swiped a fish right out of its talons, the bay is serene.

So Burroughs, with many another like-minded admirers impatient with nostalgia, joined the Friends of Merrymeeting Bay. Burroughs doesn't need to imagine what Merrymeeting Bay was to the Red Clay People or the Abnaki or Raleigh Gilbert. He writes seeing what it is:

> *There are ospreys, eagles, harriers, and once, slanting down on a long diagonal, a peregrine falcon. I saw it*

disappear into the marsh momentarily, then rise, regain altitude with choppy, powerful strokes, and head for the horizon. I paddled over to where the hawk had stooped and found a hen mallard. She floated high and dry, buoyant as a cork, her feathers unmussed and her head so neatly removed it looked as though she'd been born that way.

RUSTICATION

Islesboro is a skinny ten-mile-long island running southwest to northeast through Penobscot Bay, a few miles offshore from Camden at its southernmost and from Castine at its northeast shore. A considerable length of Maine's upper midcoast keeps Islesboro as a reference point, and it has long been a desirable destination for cruisers and day-trippers, although the island's first recorded visit by a European, the French explorer and monk André Thevet, was abruptly cut short when his party's dinner host, a sagamore of the Abnaki tribe, used as decorative ornaments the recently severed heads of six warriors of an enemy tribe.

Since then Islesboro has been the setting of many a wedding and coming-out party featuring old families from Boston, New York, and Philadelphia. It had the first planned development of rusticators at the end of the nineteenth century, subdivided waterfront plots of generous dimension sold for the purpose of having built upon them mansions or, as the previous builders of castle-size cottages liked to sneer, "starter mansions." The pastoral grace of the island was calculated from the start, and automobiles were barred in favor of horse-drawn carriages until 1934, when the six hundred or so winter residents waited till the summer swells departed after Labor Day to vote to allow cars on Islesboro.*

During the early summer of 1970 we spent a few weeks on Ducktrap Cove, a few miles up Route 1 from Camden. At nearby Lincolnville Beach we'd drive onto the car ferry with our young boys and enjoy the adventure of a gorgeous crossing of twenty minutes or so to Islesboro, putting us ashore at Grindel Point, adjacent

---

* As on many of Maine's prettier resort islands, friction between natives and newcomers is an old story. In *A Cruising Guide to the Maine Coast* the Tafts quote Michael Kinnicutt, whose distinguished family has come to Dark Harbor since the dawn of rustication, when the family would entrain from New York on the Bar Harbor Express a couple of days before Independence Day. Mr. Kinnicutt tells about a private steam yacht having dropped anchor off Dark Harbor within view of a salmon fisherman, busy setting his nets. Someone on the yacht waved the fisherman to approach, and the fisherman rowed over. "A fancy fellow climbed into the boat and told the fisherman to take him ashore. As they approached the shore, the passenger said, 'My name is George Washington Childe Drexel and I just bought that land and intend to build a large house with stables.' The fisherman squarely regarded the passenger and replied, 'My name is George Robeson, and this is my punt.'"

to a pretty white lighthouse with wildflowers growing around it. We'd drive to one end or the other of the island—out to Turtle Head, across from Castine, or past Dark Harbor and down to Bracketts Harbor, overlooking the Camden Hills, humped blue and soft to the west—and eat a picnic lunch. This was when we decided that, however we got there, Maine was for us. I remember beyond everything the quiet. Priscilla and I would perch on the rocks and Justin would dare to put his toes in the icy water and Nick would be bent at the waist, staring amazed into a tide pool, struck dumb by whatever was stirring.

In subsequent years we sailed around Islesboro's tortured coastline, threading through Bracketts Channel, past Minots Island and Tumbledown Dick; we anchored overnight at Turtle Head Cove when the wind was southeast and at Gilkey Harbor when it went northwest. We brought the dinghy ashore to eat lunch at Dark Harbor on the stone terrace of the Islesboro Inn, and if renting or buying there was beyond our reach, we thought of Islesboro as a sanctuary, just difficult enough to reach to keep it safe, and we kept a proprietary eye on it. After all, its lighthouse and pebbled beaches, memorializing one son's earliest steps and another's seduction by the sea and its edges, was frozen in our family photo album.

So it was with dismay that I learned that Islesboro in the 1990s had become the object of attention of the Hollywood diocese of Scientology. Actor Kirstie Alley* bought an estate there, and John Travolta** bought the very mansion—forty-two rooms of it, twenty bedrooms on eighty acres overlooking Sabbathday Harbor—that George Washington Childe Drexel had boasted of, with stables. "It's a retreat," in the words of Mrs. Travolta, Kelly Preston. "It's so private and pristine. Our time in Maine is special because it is a very Norman Rockwell existence."

Or a Sky King adventure. In 1992, residents of the Spruce Creek section of the island sued Travolta, an avid pilot, to prevent him from continuing to land his Gulfstream II jet on the runway in front of his house. Six years later Travolta buzzed his house in a Boeing

* A periwinkle fisherman "sucking snails" off Dark Harbor warned his friends via his website—using the handle Salty Dog—"BEWARE THE RICH FOLK!!" He cheerfully explains: Kirstie Alley was being taken in her boat from Islesboro to the Mainland. "Well, I made the mistake of passing her with my beat-up old dive boat and taking the prime spot on the public dock to unload my winkles. Well, she didn't have anything nice to say about my boat, me, or fishing folk and wanted me to move my boat to the end of the dock so it wasn't near hers! Well, needless to say I told her that if she didn't have anything nice to say, then she shouldn't say anything at all, and I was not about to move my boat till I was done! ... Oh yeah, DON'T COOK WINKLES IN THE MICROWAVE!!! pop poP pOP POP!!!"

** Maine keeps a weather eye on its Islesboro celebs: *Down East* magazine put Travolta on its December 2001 Naughty List for Santa, "for being stopped for speeding on his way to a fast-food restaurant in Rockport."

707, making three passes at it, "shaking neighboring homes," as the newspapers reported. This he had done to please his son, Jett, as his wife explained. "Most of the people we spoke to were thrilled by the experience," Kelly Preston said. "They certainly didn't tell us they were terrified. We are under the impression that it was only one or two people who complained. John just wanted to show Jett that he was at the controls of a large jet plane." In 1998 the FAA assured citizens of Islesboro that it would investigate. Uh-huh. Matt Drudge reported recently that Travolta has bought from QANTAS for eighty million dollars a 440-seat 747 jumbo jet. His spokesman explained that in this way, when the star flies—say, to the coast of Maine—"he gets to choose who gets on board with him."

Choosing better friends is the current undertaking of Islesboro's taxpayers. The meteoric rise of property values has resulted in huge property tax bills, for natives as well as rusticators. More than half a million dollars in county property taxes is paid to Waldo County, which returns very little by way of services. (The county sends only a daytime sheriff's deputy over on the ferry during summer weekends, but Islesboro is being asked to pay a big share of the county's proposed eighteen-million-dollar jail.) So the voters of Islesboro are seeking to align themselves with Knox County—which includes North Haven,

Vinalhaven, Matinicus, and Isle au Haut—if they can persuade Knox County to adopt them. This puts the neighbors of Drexels and such in the plaintive situation of the orphans of melodrama, making themselves cute when the adoption agency brings clients to look over what's available. From their perspective, the six-hundred natives are being priced out by fourteen-hundred newcomers and robbed by thousands of mainlanders. "Having one John Travolta or Kirstie Alley is a pleasant novelty," in the words of a recent online editorial in the Midcoast *VillageSoup Times*. Having an island full of them at the expense of its natives would be to create a gated community. Waterfront property taxes are soaring everywhere along the Maine coast, having more than doubled in the past five years. Islesboro's share of Waldo County's taxes has gone up 46 percent since 2002. If "summer money" can afford this, the people employed by summer money can't. "We've got to do something," the owner of the Bee's Knees Café told the *New York Times* in November 2004. "A normal person can't afford to live here anymore." The school population—the miner's canary for Maine's offshore communities—has already dropped from 106 to 83 children since 2000.

Secession is improbable at best and probably impossible. State governments—certainly Maine's—fret openly about the consequence of having communities shop around for the best deal they can broker with an adjacent county. "Opening a can of worms," one legislator calls it. "Opening the gates," says another, mordantly evoking a gated community. And as Islesboro's citizens have spent hundreds of thousands of dollars battling Waldo County in court, Waldo County has fought back with its own lawyers, and guess who pays them?

THE DIVERGENCE OF INTERESTS BETWEEN NATIVES AND rusticators "from the west'ard" (as natives sometimes put it) rarely comes down to a matter as geographically specific as tax districting. More often relations are skinned by cultural frictions. The grand nabob who doesn't pay his boatyard bills, the grande dame who upbraided the Bar Harbor local whose mongrel had had his way with her Pekinese bitch, the yachtsman demanding to be rowed ashore—these are cartoons not much different from the canny Down Easters caricatured by *Bert and I.* What Samuel Eliot Morison nicely terms the "millionaire invasion" of Mount Desert identifies only one aspect of the serial coming over and coming up of visitors with their particular reasons for coveting and exploiting and celebrating the coast of Maine. On Mount Desert painters were followed by clergymen and college professors, who were followed by bishops and college presidents. At first the newcomers and their families indulged simple ambitions: strenuous walks and strenuous conversation. But as far back as 1895, in "The Evolution of a Summer Resort," Edwin Lawrence Godkin was writing of the end of the simple old days on Mount Desert. These were the days before the proprietors of boardinghouses became the owners and managers of grand hotels, those enterprises whose magnificence was soon eclipsed by the Lucullan constructions of the Cottager, "who has become to the boarder what the red squirrel is to the gray, a ruthless invader and exterminator." Godkin noted the attendant evils of the class system, "one of which looks down on the other." The Cottager outbuilds his neighbor and clear-cuts his view from the heights to the sea—"Why," asked the radio tycoon Atwater Kent, "spoil a million-dollar view with a hundred-dollar tree?"

Of course, even then the two classes looked down on the other. But let Godkin warm to his work:

> More cottages are built, with trim lawns and private lawn-tennis grounds.... Then the dog-cart with the groom in buckskin and boots, the Irish red setter, the saddle-horse with the banged tail, the phaeton with the two ponies, the young men in knickerbockers carrying imported racquets, the girls

The great Bar Harbor fire of 1947—begun evidently
by the malign focus of the sun's rays through the windshield of a car abandoned at a local dump—brought to
an end the "monarchial" pretenses of one part of
coastal Maine. And indeed, for every overreaching
Martha Stewart in Seal Harbor there have been a dozen
Rockefellers buying up the best of Mount Desert to
give to the public. The Rockefeller family's most
recent undertaking in Maine has been to preserve
coastal farmland. A couple of years ago I attended a
benefit barbecue on the family's Bartlett Island, in
Blue Hill Bay. In 1973, David and Peggy Rockefeller
had bought the island, adjacent to Mount Desert, to
save it from development. Now it's a working farm,
impeccably unpretentious, with a herd of Simmental
cattle grazing to the water's edge. The barbecue was a
soft sell, very farmy and sweet, but a visitor might
notice that the valet parking on Mount Desert was
managed professionally by parkers from Rockefeller
Center, and that we were ferried to Bartlett Island
aboard Hinckley picnic boats that can be bought for as

little as half a million dollars. And the Simmental bull had been shampooed.

Cultural—as opposed to class—tension between rusticators and natives will not ease without effort. A promising initiative has been tried Down East in a little pamphlet published in 2004 by the lobster fishing communities of Beals and Jonesport on Moosabec Reach. It is addressed to those from away, and declares itself at once with a title: "This is not a promotional brochure." It disavows apostrophes to "sparkling water and the imagined taste of fresh lobster on the plate." It invites visitors and would-be landholders to use their senses, to learn to distinguish (as they're wakened before daybreak by the lobster fleet) "the difference between the high whine of a Detroit [diesel and] the low rumble of a Caterpillar." These newcomers are warned that the diesels may set dogs to barking, "and then your dog to respond." Gulls will shriek and later "pull apart your compost pile, steal chicken off the outdoor grill ... while depositing their 'business' on your deck furniture." The view of the working waterfront will be cluttered with traps and lines. "Also, in front of costly shorefront property, the clam and worm diggers will be working the flats when the tide is out." It smells unattractive when the tide is out. "To fishermen the smell of bait is the smell of money." Diesel fumes have their bouquet, as do lobster pounds and salmon pens. Of course, on many if not most days the visitor can touch the thick fog and will feel the unpaved roads "after a few wheel alignments, cracked windshields," and loosened fillings. "The tang of the salt air reaches your lips while you comb the beach for shells, but if you do not conserve fresh water, salt water will be pouring from your tap as well." No suburban lawns or daily car washes along Moosabec Reach. If that's okay—if you're willing to wait without honking behind a truck stopped "yes, in the middle of the road for a quick chat, to discuss the catch, to plan the next morning's departure"—then give Moosabec Reach a try.

CRUISING: PULPIT HARBOR

If one were to single out one perfect anchorage along this coast, the default destination of anyone traveling for pleasure in a boat between Casco Bay and Mount Desert, Pulpit Harbor—a hidey-hole on the northwest coast of the island of North Haven—would be that anchorage. Since the 1930s all revised editions of *The Cruising Guide to the New England Coast* have commended the star-shaped harbor: "When the skipper from busy Long Island or sandy Cape Cod furls his mainsail in Pulpit Harbor and contemplates the granite shores, the skyline spiked with spruce, the sunset behind Pulpit Rock and the Camden Hills, he can say he has truly arrived." The muddy ground holds as many as a hundred boats. The entrance, difficult to spy approaching from Penobscot Bay, is seemingly blocked by Pulpit

Rock, on whose peak perches an enormous and well-inhabited osprey nest, in use for more than two centuries, sheltering one of the oldest families in Maine. This nest has been tended by successive generations of vigorous leaseholders, each faithfully repairing and improving its inheritance, holding on for dear life in the depressed years before Rachel Carson's *Silent Spring* came to the rescue. The *Embassy Cruising Guide* to the Maine coast is downright poetic about the site, noting reassuringly that the "summer population has stabilized over several generations. This quiet harbor with elegant houses is the perfect place to watch the sun set ... while the nesting ospreys preach a whistling sermon from the guardian Pulpit Rock."

Continuity is one of the more compelling pleasures of Pulpit Harbor. Anchored here and there around the harbor are displayed recently launched examples of boatbuilding arts that were thirty-five years ago as near to extinction as Maine's raptors. With World War II had come the mass production of vessels, and after the war standardized tubs of plastic and plywood threatened to put fine woodworkers out of the boat business. Thank capitalism, I guess, for pumping enough discretionary money into big spenders' hands, beginning in the 1980s, to revive the market for huge sailing yachts and wooden boats of all sizes. There are now scores of boatbuilders thriving along the Maine coast, and the Wooden Boat School in Brooklin is only one of many institutions teaching the fine arts of bending and fitting and joining. Builders use steel and aluminum, cold-molded wood, epoxies, and traditional strip-planking to build sailing and powerboats that would inspire envy in a robber baron. When the stock market suffered its hangover following the dot-com binge, my second pang (after self-pity waned) was to lament what must surely be the end of the renaissance of ruinously expensive craftsmanship that had been commissioned while the party raged. Not at all, I learned: The patrons of yacht builders are what one boatbuilder termed "indestructibly rich." What young Maine workers learned as apprentices just in time, before their grandfathers retired, seems safely booming.

Windjammers—restored or replicated coastal schooners, mostly home-ported in Camden and Rockland—invariably make their way here for an overnight visit. These vessels, taking aboard paying passengers for a cruise of a week or less, are inelegantly known as "head boats." A cynic might resent the sound of enthusiastically off-key sea chanteys wafting from the cockpit of the *Victory Chimes,* or "Red Sails in the Sunset" whining from a squeezebox. (The jazz tenor saxman Al Cohn once defined a gentleman as someone who can play the accordion, but doesn't.) But the pretty schooners *Mary Day, Surprise, Mistress, Nathaniel Bowditch,* and *Stephen Taber* are pretty difficult to work up a case against.

So it came as a surprise a few years ago to learn the story of the unhappy and luckless Neal Parker, 45, captain of the sixty-seven-foot head boat *Wendameen,* out of Rockland. He spent fifteen thousand dollars in legal fees successfully defending himself against Coast Guard charges, threatening his commercial license, of carrying black powder aboard his ship without proper authorization and of discharging a blank charge, directed at the water, from an antique starter's pistol. Witnesses agree on the following: During the early evening hours of July 25, 2001, while the passengers and crew of the *Wendameen* were enjoying a pre-sunset supper in the cockpit, there came into Pulpit Harbor, riding an Arctic Cat 770 Jet Ski, one Ryan Maves, twenty years old. Since the principal attraction of Pulpit Harbor is its tranquility, a Jet Ski is an unwelcome intrusion. Mr. Maves, frustrated in not finding a companion in a neighboring harbor for the purpose of "super-tubing" (towing someone hitched to an inner tube at high speed and high decibels and creating tsunami-scaled wake), descended in ill-humor upon the bucolic scene in Pulpit Harbor. He "flew" in, did some doughnuts around other anchored vessels, and—noticing Captain Parker gesturing to him to slow down—buzzed the *Wendameen*. Mr. Maves then turned his attention to a low bridge near the head of the harbor, near which several children were swimming, and he "plowed" under its span back and forth, in general frightening the horses and raising strong feelings among the *Wendameen*'s passengers. He then turned his Arctic Cat toward the *Wendameen* and throttled right up to the red line, bearing down. Captain Parker, feeling his vessel and her passengers to be in distress, fired a blank round at the water (see for plausible justification Rule 7 of the Coast Guard's Navigation Rules for International Inland Waters), and Mr. Maves gave way, thinking, as he later reported to the *Bangor Daily News,* "Oh my God, I better boogie." The warring captains exchanged words. "He told me I was a menace and a nuisance," Mr. Maves said. "We made quite the threats to each other."

Captain Parker recollected in court that Mr. Maves shouted at him over his shoulder: "This is my harbor. I live here."

So many collisions in this little encounter: between classes (emblemized by Jet Ski versus stately schooner), what is meant by an "old family," what is meant by "my harbor." Pulpit Harbor has a lively history of who lived there before the people who now live there. The cruising guides unfailingly applaud the anchorage for its attractive setting among gorgeous summer cottages, bigger than they look, placed artfully among meadows, covered with clapboards or shingles, white or gray or a soft, weathered yellow, with dark green or black shutters; there's a red house with a red barn that photographs especially well. Adirondack chairs have been placed with calculated randomness around the meadow's wildflowers to favor a view to the west. As the Tafts' *Cruising Guide to the Maine Coast* remarks of one of the harbor's inner reaches, "The land surrounding this cove has been owned for generations by the Cabot family, and it is known locally as Cabot Cove." This seems just about right: If it weren't spoken for by Cabots, it might be the summer compound of Lowells or Biddles or Cadwalleders or Codmans or Crowninshields, the dilatory domicile of those who look down their noses at those who look down their noses. Pulpit Harbor is just about as tasteful as an upper-class nest can get. But hidden in the Tafts' "for generations" is a question: How long ago did this old family settle here? Cabot Cove was previously known as Wooster Creek. Where's Wooster gone to? Do you think Mr. Maves might be descended from a Wooster?

North Haven lies across from Vinalhaven on Fox Islands Thorofare, with Eggemoggin Reach and Somes

Sound one of the three most cherished cruising grounds in Maine. Because of its narrowness, with large land-masses on both sides, Fox Islands Thorofare is frequently fog-free while Penobscot Bay at either end of the seven-mile passage is socked in. Although Vinalhaven has its own millionaires' row of waterfront cottages, North Haven is Nabob Central, determinedly unshowy in a Boston/Philadelphia Main Line manner. No fancy cars, and the yacht club, the North Haven Casino, is a good deal more serious about teaching kids to sail than about dancing to Lester Lanin. The Casino, ferry wharf, and grocery store are located on the Thorofare, across North Haven and southeast of Pulpit Harbor. But when the island began to thrive in the late eighteenth and early nineteenth centuries, Pulpit Harbor was its commercial center, handy to a good supply of fresh water at Fresh Pond, with which it was connected by a millrace that powered sawmills and a gristmill. There was an active and aggressive fishing fleet, most notably of speedy mackerel schooners that expressed fresh fish to Boston's Catholic immigrants in time for meatless Fridays. Several boatbuilding sheds serviced this fleet. Philip W. Conkling's *Islands in Time* quotes a local historian on the industry and prosperity of Pulpit Harbor during the nineteenth century: "Around the Harbor there have been five stores, two fish processing plants, at least six wharves, three boat shops, a cooper shop, four mills, a church, a school, Union Hall, two post offices, and a cemetery."

In the late 1880s the mackerel fishery crashed, probably owing to overfishing. The locals began selling their land to those indestructibly rich families whose houses now look down on a harbor without a fish processing plant or gristmill or sawmill or school or—to be sure!— Union Hall. As Conkling writes, during the end of the nineteenth and beginning of the twentieth centuries "the rusticators began transforming the harbor into a pastoral landscape by removing its working waterfront." The icehouse was taken down, the fish house burned; the store was removed to Vinalhaven; the schoolhouse, built in 1867, was torn down in 1918, culminating "three decades of bad years for the North islanders, leaving a bitter legacy that reaches down to the present on the island.... I am aware of no other island where so much cultural history was removed—burned, demolished, and taken away—to re-create in its place a pastoral vision of a preindustrial coast."

The ospreys—blessings on them—held out. But what will happen to my coastal Maine—uneasily balanced between outsiders like myself and currently prosperous lobstermen—in the event of a crash of the lobster stock as cataclysmic as the mackerel dropout of the 1880s or the near extinction of the Maine cod fishery a hundred years later? After an up-and-down history of lobster catches, between the late 1940s and late 1980s the annual landing of lobsters stabilized between seventeen and twenty-five-million pounds. Then, suddenly, the harvest began to spike, increasing annually to its historic 2003 high of sixty-two-million pounds. Reasons for this phenomenon have been offered: Big cod, now gone, ate little lobsters. Sea urchins, prized by the Japanese and fished to near extinction, were no longer there to eat the kelp that lobsters use to hide from enemies. No one believed very avidly in these theories.

Lobstermen, politicians, and scientists are in agreement that a precipitous tumble is coming; the only questions are when and how bad? If the 2005 catch was only half of the 2003 catch, it would still be almost twice the mean of the latter half of the twentieth century. James Wilson, a professor of marine sciences and resource economics at the University of Maine, estimates that the average value of the annual lobster take to each of Maine's 6,500 fishermen is $100,000. To haul that many requires the interplay of two uncertain variables: stock and effort. The stock—at least above Cape Cod, below which shell disease has decimated the southern New England and Long Island Sound lobster fishery— is almost grotesquely abundant. By videotaping the

Gulf of Maine's bottom in the areas of dense lobster trap concentrations, scientists have learned that crowds of lobsters visit traps, eat bait, shelter themselves from predators, and leave, pretty much at will, to visit another trap. To be caught visiting is evidently a function of bad luck or overconfidence on the part of the lobster. And even if caught, odds are good that the unlucky crustacean will be returned to the sea, because it is too small or too large, or is a female bearing eggs or a female that once bore eggs and whose tail was notched by a previous lobsterman to protect it.

Lobstermen for the most part have seemed responsive to scientists' and resource planners' anxieties. Inuits, centuries ago, honored during times of plenty their tribal historians' warnings of coming dearth. These cycles of feast and famine were gradual enough in their playing out—perhaps a century and more—that it required faith for a tribe enjoying a bounty of blubber and sealskins and polar bear hides to begin, at the height of the good times, to tighten their belts and save for the future. There are signs of a similar tribal anxiety along the Maine coast. Increasing their effort to catch more and more lobsters, fishermen are building bigger and faster lobster boats, equipped with more sophisticated bottom scanners, radar units, hauling mechanisms. Such a vessel might cost $250,000; given the current abundance, a fisherman with a license to set hundreds of traps might secure a generous loan—say, $220,000—at low interest rates. As long as the bonanza continued, bank and fishermen would be happy. In fact, fishermen—fearing the coming depression of stock—regularly pay up front cash for more than half the price of their equipment, buying themselves buffer from the repo men.

Another hopeful component of the curious anxiety provoked by Maine's overabundance has been increasing communication—and even trust—between lobstermen and marine scientists. It has not always been thus: James Wilson was chased off of Vinalhaven at gunpoint by some mean old cobs who didn't want to hear his opinions. Years later, when I met him in 2005, Carl Wilson (James's son), the lobster expert at Maine's Department of Marine Resources in Boothbay Harbor, had just returned from a fruitful talk with the leaders of the Vinalhaven fleet. Uncertainty has yoked scientists and fishermen: Carl Wilson has said that "we definitely see a storm cloud on the horizon." These fall-offs happen fast: "You watch a resource build for two decades, and then it just drops."

Why? Questions are being asked, the water temperature monitored, the Gulf of Maine's currents charted, the water salinity measured, the origins of larval lobsters tracked, the practices of catchers and caught observed—all of this is being done, with patience and persistence. With frustration, too, because as James Wilson has testified: "We don't have (and probably never will have) the scientific ability to know exactly the right thing to do."

THE VIEW FROM OUR DOCK

Just because the kittens were born in the oven
doesn't make them biscuits.
—DOWN EAST WISDOM

We have sailed Maine often enough to know how little of it we'll ever know. Before we got *Blackwing* and began coasting regularly, we chartered sailboats out of Camden and Blue Hill. We chartered the lobster-yachtish *Skyfair* out of Bucks Harbor on Eggemoggin Reach in order to cover more water, to poke our noses east of Schoodic. We bought a twenty-one-foot Boston Whaler to go up and down its glorious rivers. We reasoned we were doing research, exploring for some perfect place someday to settle. Several years ago we began to think seriously in the present tense about living in Maine. We rented, always on the water and always beyond our means: at Ducktrap Cove and on North Haven (a house with a dock on Fox Islands Thorofare). I've mentioned the summers in Castine, a town that cast a spell. One of its many virtues is its setting so far from the clotted traffic and cheapjackery of Route 1. One of its vices was the same: It requires a drive of forty-five minutes each way to buy a pipe wrench to tighten *Blackwing*'s stuffing box. Nevertheless, we almost made an offer on a tiny house set right on the beach at Wadsworth Cove, like a serf's dwelling in the shadow of the very house—grand on a bluff above the cove—where I had spent my first night in Maine. (We couldn't afford it.) We rented a great ark of a Victorian, with its own boathouse, in East Boothbay, on the west bank of the Damariscotta River, looking across to South Bristol and Christmas Cove. We rented a cute little house on Barters Island, perched above the Back River of the Sheepscot, across the street from the bridge keeper's shack on the west end of the swing bridge to Hodgdon Island, the very bridge featured in Todd Field's 2001 movie based on an Andre Dubus story, "In the Bedroom." The best lobster rolls I've ever eaten come from the Trevett Store (which also figures in that movie), at the other end of that bridge. Priscilla sometimes helped the bridge keeper lower the warning gate and stop traffic when the keeper had to turn the crank that swings open the contraption.

Justin and Nick went to Bowdoin, and both lived in Maine after they left. Nick lives there now, first renting along the Damariscotta River in Boothbay and later buying in Bath. He and Heidi are marine biologists: He does research at the University of Southern Maine in Portland on lobsters in their larval stage, and she works at Bigelow Marine Laboratory in Boothbay Harbor on an innovative sea-data collection system of moored buoys, GoMoos (Gulf of Maine Ocean Observing System). Both my sons and their wives tried San Francisco, and Justin and Megan settled for a time in San Diego. But they were pulled back east, Justin and Megan to Cambridge, and they mean to stay east. I can't resist believing that Nick's calling was settled back when he turned three, out on Islesboro, bending over those tide pools staring and staring. Justin is an art historian, interested especially in American painting of the nineteenth century, and I believe that the pictures he looked at in Maine—the impressions made on him by Winslow Homer and Thomas Cole and Frederic Church and Edward Hopper—these sights took his heart.

The mid-coast of Maine gradually became our family's gathering place, and when Heidi and Nick had Ivan—named for Kenny Eaton's sidekick, Heidi's boat-deprived grandfather Ivan Nelson—Priscilla and I bought a little house on the river north of Bath on the west side of the Kennebec. The idea is that we'll roost there. But as for claiming kin with Maine, assuming deed to a piece of its heart? Not likely. A couple of summers back, I walked downriver to the Bath Iron Works for the launching of the yard's twenty-third Aegis Class destroyer, the *Momsen* (DDG 92), named for a legendary World War II–era submariner, Charles Bower "Swede" Momsen. These destroyers are ferally graceful, and scooting past it in our outboard, keeping well outside the security perimeter patrolled by harbor police, I had admired its evolution from stark plates of steel and aluminum to sea-ready ship of the line.

A few blocks north of BIW I came across picketing protesters from several church and antiwar disarmament groups. It was August 9, 2003, the fifty-eighth anniversary of the date we dropped "Fat Man" on Nagasaki. One of the leaflets I was given by a picketer explained that "we raise our voices in opposition to the ongoing preparations for war in Maine. We know that we do not need to go to Iraq to find Weapons of Mass Destruction." The U.S.S. *Momsen* would be equipped with fifty-six Tomahawk missiles, and each missile, if nuclear-tipped, could visit destruction equivalent to sixteen Nagasaki bombs. In addition, the *Momsen* would be armed with Harpoon surface-to-surface missiles and with the Evolved Seasparrow defensive missile system.

With her depth chargers and big guns and tracking systems, this was a serious destroyer. Previous Bath-built warships were among the armada that began the "shock and awe" bombardment of Baghdad five months earlier.

It was also a beautiful ship, rakish and handsomely proportioned, with a sharp bow entry and lissome beam and a superstructure bristling with mysteries. I wanted to see her up close. As I approached the main gate, picketers were chanting from the sidewalk across the street, and a guard at the gate pointed across the street, as though to tell me to go to them. At first I didn't understand. In an earlier life I was a journalist, and I was accustomed to covering protests rather than joining them. I explained to the guard that I lived in Bath, but he didn't believe me, and when I showed him my ID, a California driver's license, he believed me even less. He told me to cross the street or leave. Very polite he was, but willing to point out that my green T-shirt (my navy blue shirt was in the washing machine) and my white beard were all the ID he needed. So there in No Mans Land it dawned on me that I was destined to be no one's man.

Now I'm down at my dock, before breakfast. My grandson Ivan's with me. I don't know whether he'll become a biscuit. He's two, Maine-born and Bath-raised.

He does what the other kids in this town—the children of pacifists, police officers, BIW welders, and armorers—do: listens to stories being read aloud at the Patten Free Library, watches Little League games at the Lincoln Street field, dreams of belting a frozen-rope liner over the fence. Ivan sits on Santa's lap at City Hall and marches in the Halloween parade. He runs along the tideline at Popham Beach, and bends over to stare at something stirring in the water.

After the tourists leave, and the leaves fall, and the snowbirds line up at the post office to send cartons to Punta Gorda and Bradenton, the winding-down is a novelty. The cold turns sharp and it hurts some mornings to breathe. The first snow falls in October, and then November makes you recollect what you learned about the Pophamites who wintered over just downstream a bit. You buy insulated Sorel boots at Reny's. The gray sky presses down on the gray river, like an iron lid on an iron kettle. Sleet drums against the windows. Night falls a few minutes after lunch, and you begin to miss the Red Sox. There's not much to do except read and talk and listen to jazz, and you wonder whether it might not be foresightful to reserve tickets in Fort Meyer during spring training.

But this morning it's freezing. Capt. Dave Dooley, who built our dock, removes its float and ramp in the winter to save them from the depredations of Kennebec ice. From the dock's platform I can see across to Days Ferry. It's pretty on the east side of the river, pacific. It's hard to imagine the misery over there during the bad old days of the French and Indian wars. I think I understand why a band of Abnaki warriors crept up on the Hammonds—the natives were aggrieved, of course—but my grandson is standing right here, pointing at something, and I wish the braves hadn't killed the Hammond father and son right over there across from my house, and then marched the mother and her little kids to Quebec to sell as slaves to the French. I wish a lot of things hadn't happened along this pretty river, and to my country at Pearl Harbor and the World Trade Center, and to Hiroshima and Nagasaki and Iraq in my country's name.

An American of my generation—born shortly before World War II and growing up with industrial progress, housing developments, highways, billboards, toxic rhetoric, unfelt compassion, dead rivers—is unaccustomed to happy stories about our treatment of our planet. It can become a reflex to assume the inexorability of abuse, that our backyards will surely go to hell or be condemned, maybe because they've gone toxic or because they'll be useful to a shopping mall. To think of the commons is too easily to think of its tragedy. It's difficult to break these cheerless and depreciating habits. But I know that Captain Dooley takes fishing parties out every summer day, usually twice a day, and that he and his guests can't stop catching stripers and throwing them back for someone else to catch. More dams will come down on the Kennebec, are coming down on other rivers in Maine. I know this, but I still can't credit my senses. It will be different for Ivan; his senses will be trained by this wonderful, repaired river.

He's pointing with his mitten to something out there. Something's moving; it's not a skater, because there was a thaw a couple of days ago, and the ice has fractured into floes ebbing down toward Doubling Point and Popham and out to Seguin. Something's stirring on one of the floes, a menacing shadow, and then another shadow, and then—gliding in for a landing— our very own eagles, one of them with a fish. And on that chunk of ice they float, like summer idlers on a party boat, languidly dipping their white heads as they tear into their smelt, breakfast on the Kennebec, at home in Maine.

A NOTE TO THE READER

For titles of some books, the definite article is a presumption if not a falsehood. I'll concede that *The Edge of Maine* is such an instance. Not principally because this state has three edges in addition to its coast, but because the jagged line I've tried to draw through space and time is so bent and discontinuous. Even to assign an indefinite article—an edge—is a reach. An edge of *my* Maine would approximate accuracy, but with such a solipsistic title what book could have brought you as far as this confession? Maybe if I admit to having had a bad dream in which my title became *My Dull Edge of Maine,* reviewers will leave that arrow in their quivers.

Reviewers are on my mind. I think of any Maine-experienced reader of this book as a reviewer, a person having strong feelings about the words a visitor chooses to describe what he sees. And of what that visitor has seen, what does he choose to describe? What has he seen but failed to observe, or observed but failed to comprehend? Even the most liberal of readers will notice what I've sailed past in the fog: The Isles of Shoals, Casco Bay, Portland, Muscongus Bay, Eggemoggin Reach, Winter Harbor, Roque Island. And of course much of what captured my interest in the telling of this story I got at second- and third-hand, from books and magazines, photos and newspapers. Having been drawn to this project by personal encounters, I often found the accounts of others more invigorating than my memories.

Some reviewers are professional guardians of Maine, or perhaps their "edge of Maine." Thus, for instance, Sanford Phippen, born in 1942 in Hancock, on Frenchman Bay near Mount Desert, worked as a boy for summer rusticators, mowing lawns and delivering milk and eggs. He went to the University of Maine at Orono and stayed put. As a Maine writer he has undertaken to review books about his state, some written by natives who might nonetheless be sightseers to the time in history their books explore, or to the exotic offshore island they describe. Louise Dickinson Rich was one such. E. B. White, removing his attention from Manhattan to Brooklin was another. Having reviewed "several hundred books either about Maine or by Maine writers, or by people who consider themselves Maine's spokesmen," Phippen writes that he feels akin to Federico Fellini, who remarked that he read books about Rome to "forget what Rome was like." And this condemnation doesn't even include the efforts of out-and-out strangers from away.

Phippen complains that the superficial Maine that he reads is the fabulation of "Maine Mythologists" and "Year-Round Summer People," prettied and patronized, lacking in realism, lacking the "poverty, solitude, struggle, lowered aspirations" of "living on the edge." His proprietary dismay is amplified by George H. Lewis, a professor of sociology and anthropology who makes a systematic tour (in *The Journal of American Culture*) of "The Maine That Never Was: The Construction of Popular Myth in Regional Culture." Having studied brochures and pamphlets from tourist bureaus and railroads and resorts and chambers of commerce, Lewis contrasts the rouged and powdered and jolly and sunstruck postcards with the punishing statistical realities of daily life in year-round Maine. Unsurprisingly, Maine, like everywhere else on the planet, is not fun for all, or even for most. The license plate that celebrates our territory— "Vacationland," adorned by a driver's choice of pinecone, lobster, or loon—advertises a myth.

Let me stipulate that the Maine I have experienced and attempted to record is partial, as in biased and incomplete. Carolyn Chute's *Beans of Egypt, Maine* represents, I concede, a brutish reality. The Know-Nothings burned the Catholic church in my own Bath in the mid-nineteenth century, while over in Ellsworth they tarred and feathered the Reverend John Bapst and ran him out of town on a rail. In 1924, when the Ku Klux Klan had the largest membership of any state in our nation, Maine's voters elected a Klansman governor and twenty thousand citizens marched the streets of Portland to celebrate the event. Today, OxyContin abuse is alarmingly common among subsets of Maine lobstermen. The class divide is spectacular near lakes and along the coast, though Helen Yglesias, in *Starting,* surely exaggerates in claiming that the "spread between the poor and the rich is as wide as that in any undeveloped country." Let's agree too that Maine suffers its share of Yglesias's inventory of vices and sorrows: "alcoholism, incest, illicit love, illegitimacy, … madness, … couple-switching, … vandalism and rebelliousness among adolescents." (The final defect strikes me as piquant.) Yet to insist, parochially, that Maine is specially cursed seems to me merely the mirror image of the distortion that has romanticized the state.

The Edge of Maine owes huge debts to writers who, for the most part, have been astonished by the place. Sometimes their astonishment has been provoked by dismay. To read of the tragedy that befell the infant son of the sagamore Squando, who was drowned when English trappers—testing their hypothesis that Indians swam naturally, like some animals—overturned the canoe in which the baby was being paddled by his mother, is not to experience nostalgia for a simpler time. To read about the slaughter of settlers by Squando's tribe, in retaliation, is not to romanticize the Noble Savage.

Among the many writers cited in the text, some were inspirational in tone and emphasis as well as indispensable for events, dates, and circumstances. Philip W. Conkling's writings on the islands of Maine are monumental and elegant. The Duncans—Robert and Roger S.—have made literature of cruising guides, as have the Tafts, Jan and the late Hank. Samuel Eliot Morison humanizes history on every scale, whether in his majestic view of the early explorations of North America or his intimate account of Mount Desert Island. Colin Woodard's *The Lobster Coast: Rebels, Rusticators, and the Struggle for a Forgotten Frontier* is the most recent of at least half a dozen serious studies of the persistent mystery of those cycles of feast or famine that have dramatized Maine's flamboyant history, from chimerical Norumbega through the shipbuilding bonanza and ice rush of the nineteenth century unto the current cliffhanger of next year's uncertain lobster harvest.

ABOUT THE AUTHOR

Geoffrey Wolff is the author of the acclaimed biographies *Black Sun, The Duke of Deception,* and *The Art of Burning Bridges.* His novels include *Providence* and *The Age of Consent.* Currently he is the director of the graduate fiction program at the University of California at Irvine and splits his time between California and Maine.

The interior text of this book is set in Garamond
3, designed by Morris Fuller Benton and
Thomas Maitland Cleland in the 1930s and
released digitally by Adobe.

Printed by R. R. Donnelley and Sons on
Gladfelter 60-pound Thor Offset smooth
white antique paper.

Dust jacket printed by Miken Companies.
Color separation by Quad Graphics.

Three-piece case of Ecological Fiber navy side
panels with Sierra black book cloth as the spine
fabric. Stamped in Lustrofoil metallic silver.